S. HRG. 113–384

OUTER CONTINENTAL SHELF PRODUCTION

HEARING

BEFORE THE

COMMITTEE ON ENERGY AND NATURAL RESOURCES UNITED STATES SENATE

ONE HUNDRED THIRTEENTH CONGRESS

SECOND SESSION

TO

EXAMINE OUTER CONTINENTAL SHELF PRODUCTION AND TO IDENTIFY WHAT ACTIONS THE FEDERAL GOVERNMENT CAN TAKE TO MAXIMIZE THE OPPORTUNITIES AND MINIMIZE THE CHALLENGES

LAFAYETTE, LA, JULY 7, 2014

Printed for the use of the
Committee on Energy and Natural Resources

U.S. GOVERNMENT PRINTING OFFICE

89–687 PDF   WASHINGTON : 2014

For sale by the Superintendent of Documents, U.S. Government Printing Office
Internet: bookstore.gpo.gov   Phone: toll free (866) 512–1800; DC area (202) 512–1800
Fax: (202) 512–2104   Mail: Stop IDCC, Washington, DC 20402–0001

(II)

CONTENTS

STATEMENTS

OUTER CONTINENTAL SHELF PRODUCTION

MONDAY, JULY 7, 2014

U.S. SENATE,
COMMITTEE ON ENERGY AND NATURAL RESOURCES,
Lafayette, LA

The committee met, pursuant to notice, at 1:35 p.m. at the Mardi Gras Room, Cajundome Convention Center, 444 Cajundome Boulevard, Lafayette, Louisiana, Hon. Mary Landrieu, chairwoman, presiding.

OPENING STATEMENT OF HON. MARY L. LANDRIEU, U.S. SENATOR FROM LA

The CHAIR. Good afternoon.

Let me call the Senate Natural Resources Committee of the U.S. Senate to order. Thank you all for joining us today for an official field hearing of this committee.

I am so proud to chair this committee on behalf of the people of Louisiana. When the people of Louisiana hold this gavel good things happen, in my view, for the industry, the oil and gas industry, which is so important and vibrant in our country today, our State, the Gulf Coast region and the Nation.

When our State first wielded the chairman's gavel, held by Bennett Johnston in 1987, there were significant obstacles to deep water drilling becoming the power house that it is today and actually the subject, OCS, of this field hearing. However by the time he left office after 20 years as a member of this committee and nearly 10 years as serving as chair the percentage of deep water leases had gone from 40 to 70 percent of the entire gulf. Because Senator Johnston was a Gulf Coast Senator, there have only been 2 chairs of the Energy Committee in the history of the United States from the East, both of us being from the Gulf Coast.

He was focused on expanding and growing this industry and the thousands of high paying jobs it creates. I will do the same as chair.

This February the people of Louisiana got this gavel back after waiting in line for 20 years. With this gavel now in hand I'm confident that this committee can use it in a way to expand this industry both onshore and offshore, reduce unnecessary and redundant regulations that cost time, money and jobs, build on the revenue sharing partnership that was actually established by this committee, led by myself and Senator Pete Domenici, when he chaired the committee. Also achieve American energy security for the first time in our Nation's history.

(1)

We may do that as a Nation or we may do it as a North American continent. But in our lifetime it can be done with the changes of both technological, political and otherwise that are occurring in Canada, the U.S. and in Mexico. The State of Louisiana and our offshore energy industry will play a big role in making this goal. I think this is a worthy goal, an exciting goal, a reality.

I'd like to thank all of our witnesses today for coming today. Look forward to hearing their thoughts on how Congress, the private industry and all stakeholders can work together to harness the abundant offshore revenues, both traditional and non-traditional, resources to provide real energy security for America and be a model industry for the world.

Let me go into just a few minutes in this opening statement about the history of the OCS. Then we'll hear from our panel, our first panel. Then we have a distinguished group of industry leaders for our second panel.

When our country was established America literally stopped at the water's edge. In 1973, in 1793 it was President George Washington who expanded the country and claimed all submerged areas, up to 3 miles off of our coast. If President Washington had gone further and claimed the entire Outer Continental Shelf of our 13 original colonies, he would have single handedly increased our country's land mass by 10 percent and added that much more land to the United States.

However, it took 152 years and 32 more presidents.

When Harry Truman then claimed the entire Outer Continental Shelf and the resources beneath it for the people of the United States this expanded our country's territory by 70 percent. There are resources in this land that may be under the water, but it's our land and it's our resource base. It must be harnessed and tapped to build the economy and security of the United States.

Today we are here to hear from the Department of Interior and the Department of Energy on their plans to develop this extraordinary resource.

Eight years later In 1953 Congress passed the Outer Continental Shelf's Lands Act, the first law of its kind. After President Truman claimed the Outer Continental Shelf for the U.S. Congress passed the first Outer Continental Shelf Lands Act, the first law of its kind to govern how the country would explore and harness the vast natural resources off of our shores. Twenty-five years later we updated the law and called on the Department of Interior to prepare and periodically revise a national assessment of our oil and gas leasing process on these lands.

Today that is known as the DOI, Department of Interior's, 5 year plan. Mr. Cruickshank is here to testify today as to what that plan is.

It has also called on the Secretary of Interior to establish a number of planning areas to incorporate in each plan. There are currently 26 planning areas in the Outer Continental Shelf, 15 in Alaska, 4 along the Pacific Coast, 3 in the Gulf of Mexico and 4 in the Atlantic.

Currently there are only 36 million acres, an area only slightly larger than the State of Louisiana itself, that is actively leased. So a very small portion of the Outer Continental Shelf is actively leased. That's only 2 percent of the entire OCS.

By comparison it would be as if the country stopped at Rhode Island, you know, or Vermont, you know, or whatever 2 percent of the land mass is. So there's a tremendously vast area of the Outer Continental Shelf that should be, in my view, explored and looked at for what resources it might hold, either traditional or non-traditional resources, whether energy or otherwise, for the economic benefit of our people in the United States and in the world.

The Department of Interior is currently drafting its 5 year plan for 2017 to 2022. We're currently operating on the previous 5 year plan. The process that we're beginning right now for 2017 to 2022 offers us a great opportunity to build upon the success, I believe, of the Gulf of Mexico Energy Security Act, GOMESA, an important and essential law that was passed in 2006 by working with both Republicans and Democrats, both Senate and House, led by Senator Domenici and myself.

GOMESA was the first bill passed in a long time, and possibly forever, to open up 8.3 million acres of the Gulf to oil and gas exploration since the original plan. It was the first time Congress had ever opened up so many acres to new exploration. This area would soon produce up to 2 million additional barrels of oil per day. That's more than 10 percent of what the United States consumes and more oil than we import from Saudi Arabia.

It is clear from this example that good things can happen when we open up more areas for drilling in a responsible manner. We can and should do even more, in my view, in a balanced and environmentally thoughtful way. To start we should complete an updated resources assessment of the entire OCS, particularly the areas off the East Coast.

Since 1990 our proven reserves have multiplied dramatically each time the government completes a survey. Swift new advances in drilling technology are making more of what we find easier to extract. More drilling means more energy and more high paying jobs, more security, more reliability and a stronger economy. We need to act and turn this promising potential into a reality, in my view.

Having these potential resources beneath our waters and not using them is short sighted. It makes us more dependent on countries that are unstable or countries that do not share our values. The next 5 year plan must open up more areas for energy production off of our coast.

One way to ensure that we can responsibly develop more of our offshore resources is to make the permitting process as efficient as possible. Unnecessary regulations drive innovators out of the market and prevent us from creating more high paying, energy jobs. Inefficient regulations and lack of certainty add additional cost and time into the permitting process in the Gulf compared to other areas of the world.

Since capital will flow to the areas that have the most promise, it's important, in my view, for the U.S. OCS to be one of the more promising areas and particularly the traditional OCS which is the Gulf of Mexico. Delays cause many companies to move production assets to other parts of the world like Asia and Africa. As a Louisiana Senator, of course, I want to keep as many jobs here in Louisiana, in the Gulf Coast area and in the United States as possible.

North America can be a power house. An energy secure and independent North America is something worth fighting for, working for and working across parties lines to achieve, particularly in light of the current turmoil in Iraq, ongoing Russian aggression against the Ukraine and some of its other neighbors. It has never been more important or more possible.

Considering the changes in the political landscape in a very positive way in Mexico, and Canada's continued advancement of their technologies, both on the energy side and the environmental side , it is really, truly an exciting time for us in this industry and in this particular geographic space.

For a coastal State like Louisiana, to produce more energy offshore, we must build on the revenue sharing partnership that was established with Senator Domenici through GOMESA in 2006. Before this law was passed, as everyone knows, Gulf Coast States played host to energy production offshore and our States, Louisiana, Texas, Mississippi and Alabama, that were production host States, received virtually no share of the revenues from the Outer Continental Shelf which begins only 3 miles off of our coast.

Contrary to this situation and great irritation to me and to others, the Federal Government shared 50 percent of those same revenues on Federal lands in interior States. Rentals, royalties, bonus bids were sent to the Federal Government and one half were left in States like Wyoming, New Mexico, Utah, etcetera, while 100 percent of the Gulf Coast OCS revenues were taken and deposited into the general fund of the United States. Now we changed that with GOMESA.

The Gulf has already received $31,000,000 from this law. In 2017 under the current law, these 4 States will receive up to $50,000,000 to be divided among ourselves. But without lifting the revenue sharing cap, we will not be in the same situation as the interior States which, I believe, is an equality issue that we need to work on.

That's why I'm committed to passing the FAIR Act. This committee will consider that Act very shortly. I co-sponsored this legislation with Senator Lisa Murkowski of Alaska. This bill would accelerate revenue sharing payments to the State the year of its enactment and lift the arbitrary cap of $500 million placed on the Gulf Coast States, a cap that does not exist for any other State or any other region of the country.

Allowing coastal States to share in the same or an equitable percentage, whatever Congress would believe, as the interior States would be fair. In my opinion 50 percent would be equitable. But we are open to the discussion. GOMESA is 37 and a half percent.

We can then use those revenues to keep America's working coast, America's energy coast, strong and vibrant. More of that revenue sharing would mean more lands preserved and more wildlife refuges made stronger. It could also help us to stem the tide of erosion along our coast and could be used for appropriate energy related infrastructure and development.

More offshore energy exploration and production means more high paying jobs for hard working families that pay the kind of wages that allow our middle class to grow, to buy homes, to save for the future and to build wealth. It means achieving energy security for the United States, something that has bedeviled the Members of Congress and Presidents for decades.

So today's hearing is about what we need to do to make this a reality.

Today's hearing is about what promise does the OCS hold.

What are the resources?

What is the government's plan to develop these resources?

You can see the small chart here that outlines the planning areas. Of course, there's limited capital. There's limited infrastructure. So we have to have a plan that directs resources to a certain area.

If it were all open which, you know, we could think about as well, it would be interesting to see what areas would receive the first interest from the industry. But clearly there's more land, more leases that can be opened. You know, there are different views about this. We'll hear some of those today.

But I'm happy to conduct this field hearing on behalf of the Energy and Natural Resources Committee to hear from the people on the ground here in Acadiana at the center of America's energy coast.

There will be, clearly, field hearings held in other parts of the country. There will be different kinds of testimony presented. But I believe it's important as we develop this 5 year plan to get a variety of different impacts starting with the region that does the most drilling, and supports the most production in the Outer Continental Shelf.

It is clear to me that the first hearing on the next 5 year plan should be right here in Lafayette, in South Louisiana which is the center of Gulf Coast production. I believe that my Texas and Alabama and Mississippi Senators would agree with that. Louisiana is looked on, particularly, Lafayette and this Lake Charles area, as sort of the working coast, the center of all support services for the offshore. We have most of the energy ports in the Gulf Coast.For these reasons, this is a perfect place to hold this hearing.

So at this time if Dr. Cruickshank and Mr. Sieminski would come forward to begin your testimony. As you know we've received it. We've reviewed it. You each have 5 minutes to testify.

We'll start with Dr. Cruickshank first and then go to Mr. Sieminski.

You'll be notified when you have 30 seconds to wrap up. Then I'll introduce the second panel.

Dr. Cruickshank, thank you very much. You're always welcome. You've been before our committee many times before. I understand you've been in the government service for almost or maybe 30 years. So we're happy to have you testify as a knowledgeable leader in our government.

Welcome.

STATEMENT OF WALTER CRUICKSHANK, ACTING DIRECTOR, BUREAU OF OCEAN ENERGY MANAGEMENT, DEPARTMENT OF THE INTERIOR

Mr. CRUICKSHANK. Chair Landrieu, I am pleased to appear before you today to discuss a number of important issues including the current 5 year Outer Continental Shelf Oil and Gas Leasing Program, the United States/Mexico Trans boundary Hydrocarbon Agreement and development of the next 5 year oil and gas leasing program.

The Bureau of Ocean Energy Management provides for the environmentally and economically responsible management of the Nation's energy and mineral resources on the Outer Continental Shelf. One of the primary means for doing so is the 5-year oil and gas leasing program. The current 5 year program for 2012 to 2017 schedules 15 proposed lease sales and 6 planning areas that include more than 75 percent of the estimated, undiscovered, technically recoverable oil and gas resources in Federal offshore waters.

To date, BOEM has conducted 5 lease sales, 2 in the Western Gulf of Mexico planning area, 2 in the Central Gulf of Mexico and one in that portion of the Eastern Gulf, not subject to moratorium under the Gulf of Mexico Energy Security Act.

These sales resulted in leasing approximately 4.3 million acres for a total of nearly $2.3 billion in bonus bids. The next sale in the 5-year program is in the Western Gulf of Mexico scheduled for next month. Six other lease sales are scheduled for the Gulf of Mexico through the end of the 5-year program and 3 lease sales are scheduled offshore Alaska, one each in portions of the Chukchi Sea, Beaufort Sea and Cook Inlet planning areas. The 5-year program adopted a targeted leasing strategy in the Arctic to focus leasing on the most promising blocks while protecting important Arctic habitats and critical subsistence activities.

In the mid and south Atlantic BOEM is currently pursuing a strategy to develop modern, scientific information about the scope and location of potential oil and gas resources and to resolve significant potential conflicts between oil and gas activity and other important uses of Federal waters. A record of decision that sets a framework for appropriate geological and geophysical survey activities off the mid and south Atlantic coast and that clears the way for G and G permits to be considered is expected to be issued in the coming weeks. Information gained from this data will help inform BOEM's decisions regarding potential future leasing along the Atlantic coast.

Turning to the United States Mexico Trans Boundary Hydrocarbon Agreement.

This agreement was signed into law in December of last year creating a new level of certainty for U.S. and Mexico firms operating in the Gulf Offshore Boundary region and making additional areas accessible for safe and responsible exploration and production activities. The Trans Boundary Agreement sets clear guidelines for the development of oil and natural gas reservoirs that cross the maritime boundary. Under the agreement U.S. and Mexican operators will be able to voluntarily enter into agreements to jointly develop these reservoirs.

In the event the companies can't agree the Trans Boundary Agreement establishes a process through which U.S. and Mexican operators can individually develop the resources on each side of the border while protecting each Nation's interests and resources.

The Trans Boundary Agreement enters into force on July 18th at which time the leasing moratorium on blocks within the 1.4 nautical mile buffer area, north of the boundary in the Western Gap expires and those blocks will be available for leasing.

With the current 5 year program expiring in August 2017 BOEM recently announced the first step in a robust public engagement and analytical process to develop the next 5 year program for 2017 to 2022. The OCS Lands Act requires the Secretary of the Interior to prepare and maintain a schedule of proposed oil and gas lease sales in Federal waters indicating the size, timing and location of sales that would best meet national energy needs while achieving the appropriate balance among the potential for environmental impacts for discovery of oil and gas and for adverse effects on the coastal zone.

Last month BOEM took the first step in the development of the next 5 year program with the publication of a request for information and comments.

The RFI, as it is known, is the initial step in a 2 and a half to 3 year planning process. It does not identify any specific course of action. Consistent with past practice and judicial guidance BOEM will evaluate all 26 OCS planning areas during this first planning stage.

The RFI provides an opportunity for interested parties to submit comments and suggestions about the potential for leasing and to identify environmental and other concerns and uses that may be affected by offshore leasing.

The RFI's public comment period ends on July 31st.

Using the information received in response to the RFI BOEM will prepare successive decision documents describing a draft proposed program followed by a proposed program and a proposed final program. Throughout the planning process BOEM will consult with all interested parties and seek additional public comment. Concurrently BOEM will prepare a programmatic environmental impact statement to evaluate the potential environmental impacts of various OCS oil and gas leasing alternatives and to help inform decisions on the proposed final program.

Chair Landrieu, thank you again for inviting me to appear today. I look forward to working with the committee, especially as we proceed with development of the next 5 year program. I will be happy to answer any questions you may have.

[The prepared statement of Mr. Cruickshank follows:]

PREPARED STATEMENT OF WALTER CRUICKSHANK, ACTING DIRECTOR, BUREAU OF OCEAN ENERGY MANAGEMENT, DEPARTMENT OF THE INTERIOR

Chair Landrieu and Members of the Committee, I am pleased to appear before you today to discuss a number of important issues including, the current 2012–2017 Five Year Oil and Gas Leasing Program, the United States—Mexico Transboundary Hydrocarbon Agreement, and development of the next Five Year Oil and Gas Leasing Program for 2017—2022.

2012—2017 Five Year Oil and Gas Leasing Program

The 2012—2017 Five Year Oil and Gas Leasing Program (2012—2017 Five Year Program) became effective in August 2012, and schedules lease sales in six planning areas with the greatest resource potential, including more than 75 percent of the estimated undiscovered, technically recoverable oil and gas resources on the Outer Continental Shelf (OCS) comprising nearly 219 million acres in 15 proposed lease sales.

To date, the Bureau of Ocean Energy Management (BOEM) has conducted five lease sales—two in the Western Gulf of Mexico Planning Area, two in the Central Gulf of Mexico Planning Area, and one in the portion of the Eastern Gulf of Mexico Planning Area not subject to moratorium under the Gulf of Mexico Energy Security Act. Under the current Five Year Program, approximately 4.3 million acres, including 794 tracts, have been leased for a total of nearly $2.3 billion in bonus bids. The next sale in the Five Year Program is Lease Sale 238 in the Western Gulf of Mexico Planning Area scheduled for August 2014. Six other lease sales are scheduled for the Western, Central and Eastern Gulf of Mexico Planning Areas, and three lease sales are scheduled offshore Alaska, one each in portions of the Chukchi Sea, Beaufort Sea, and Cook Inlet Planning Areas.

The 2012—2017 Five Year Program adopted a targeted leasing strategy in the Arctic to focus oil and gas leasing on the most promising blocks, while protecting important Arctic habitats and critical subsistence activities. The strategy, which includes consultations with Alaska Natives, the State, other Federal agencies, and other stakeholders, identifies areas considered for leasing that have high resource potential and clear indications of industry interest while appropriately weighing environmental protection and subsistence use needs.

BOEM is currently pursuing a specific strategy to develop modern, robust scientific information about the scope and location of potential oil and gas resources in the Mid and South Atlantic and to resolve significant potential conflicts between oil and gas activity and other important OCS uses in these areas, including military, fishing, and vessel traffic uses as well as environmental and infrastructure concerns. A Record of Decision that sets a framework for appropriate geological and geophysical (G&G) survey activities off the Mid- and South Atlantic coast and clears the way for G&G permits to be considered, is expected to be issued in the coming weeks. Information gained from this G&G data gathering will help inform BOEM's decisions regarding potential future leasing along the Atlantic coast.

United States—Mexico Transboundary Hydrocarbon Agreement

Earlier this year, BOEM issued three leases in the Western Planning Area of the Gulf of Mexico, along the United States—Mexico Maritime Boundary. The three bids were opened during the Eastern and Central Gulf of Mexico Planning Area lease sales held on March 19, 2014. The three bids totaled over $21 million and were submitted by Exxon Mobil Corporation.

The United States—Mexico Transboundary Hydrocarbon Agreement (Transboundary Agreement), signed into law on December 26, 2013, creates a new level of certainty for U.S. and Mexican firms operating in the Gulf offshore boundary region and makes additional areas accessible for exploration and production activities. The Transboundary Agreement sets clear guidelines for the development of oil and natural gas reservoirs that cross the maritime boundary. Under the Agreement, U.S. and Mexico's operators will be able to voluntarily enter into agreements to jointly develop those reservoirs. In the event that consensus cannot be reached, the Transboundary Agreement establishes the process through which U.S. and Mexico's operators can individually develop the resources on each side of the border while protecting each nation's interests and resources.

The Transboundary Agreement allows leaseholders on the U.S. side of the maritime boundary to cooperate with Mexico's operators, in the joint exploration and safe and responsible development of hydrocarbon resources. The Agreement also provides for joint inspection teams from the Bureau of Safety and Environmental Enforcement (BSEE) and the Mexican Government to ensure compliance with applicable laws and regulations. Relevant agencies in both countries will review plans for the development of these reservoirs, and additional requirements may be set before development activities are allowed to begin.

This agreement makes the entire transboundary region, which was subject to legal uncertainty in the absence of an agreement, more attractive to U.S.-qualified operators. BOEM estimates that the transboundary area contains as much as 172 million barrels of oil and 304 billion cubic feet of natural gas.

With entry into force of the Transboundary Agreement on July 18, the leasing moratoria on blocks within the 1.4 nautical mile buffer area north of the Continental Shelf boundary in the Western Gap expires, and those blocks will be available for leasing.

2017—2022 Five Year Oil and Gas Leasing Program

With the current Five Year Program expiring in August 2017, BOEM recently announced the first step in a robust public engagement and analytical process to develop the next schedule of potential offshore oil and gas lease sales.

The OCS Lands Act requires the Secretary of the Interior, through BOEM, to prepare and maintain a schedule of proposed oil and gas lease sales in Federal waters, indicating the size, timing and location of sales that would best meet national energy needs while achieving an appropriate balance among the potential for environmental impacts, for discovery of oil and gas, and for adverse effects on the coastal zone.

Last month, BOEM took the first step in the development of the next Five Year Program with the publication of a Request for Information and Comments on the Preparation of the 2017-2022 Outer Continental Shelf Oil and Gas Leasing Program (RFI). The RFI is the initial step in a two-and-a-half to three-year planning process and does not identify any specific course of action. Per statute and consistent with previous efforts and judicial guidance, BOEM will evaluate all 26 OCS planning areas during this first stage. The publication of the RFI begins a 45-day comment period ending on July 31, 2014. The RFI provides an opportunity for interested parties to submit comments and suggestions about the potential for leasing and to identify environmental and other concerns and uses that may be affected by offshore leasing. BOEM seeks a wide array of input, including information on the economic, social and environmental values of all OCS resources, as well as the potential impact of oil and gas exploration and development on other resource values of the OCS and the marine, coastal and human environments.

Substantial public involvement and extensive analysis will accompany all stages of the planning process. BOEM is reaching out to a broad array of stakeholders, including State governments, coastal organizations, and tribal representatives to educate them on BOEM's programs, policies and procedures, as well as working with the Department of Defense (DOD) to resolve potential conflicts between the OCS leasing program and DOD requirements to use the OCS for national defense and security. BOEM is holding meetings with coastal States if requested; BOEM has met with the State of North Carolina and is scheduled to meet with the Commonwealth of Virginia in early July. Additionally, in response to coastal state requests and in order to enable States to prepare a robust response to the RFI, BOEM is hosting a meeting in its Gulf of Mexico Region office in New Orleans on July 16-17 to share comprehensive information on BOEM's, as well as the Bureau of Safety Environmental Enforcement's, programs from oil and gas leasing to decommissioning activities.

Using the information received in response to the RFI, BOEM will prepare decision documents describing the Draft Proposed Program, followed by a Proposed Program and a Proposed Final Program. Throughout the planning process, BOEM consults with all interested parties and seeks additional public comment on the Draft Proposed and Proposed Programs. Concurrently, BOEM will prepare a Programmatic Environmental Impact Statement (PEIS) required by the National Environmental Policy Act to evaluate the potential environmental impacts of various OCS oil and gas leasing alternatives under the Proposed Program and to help inform decisions on the Proposed Final Program.

Permitting and Production

The aforementioned BOEM activities have the potential to increase exploration, drilling, and production on the OCS. I have been asked to mention a few significant efforts by our sister agency, the Bureau of Safety and Environmental Enforcement (BSEE). To further enhance safety and environmental protection across offshore operations, BSEE has initiated a variety of regulatory improvements to address key safety issues. As BSEE continues to evaluate possible regulatory updates, for topics such as well control processes and technologies, crane safety and oil spill response and preparedness, the bureau has also worked to streamline the regulatory process to improve efficiency, provide for more stakeholder input, and keep pace with industry as offshore activity and production increases.

Over the past few years BSEE's permit review times have decreased, without sacrificing human safety and protection of the environment. For example, BSEE achieved an average review time of 59 days for deepwater New Well permits submitted and approved in 2013, down from 71 days in 2011. BSEE has focused on reducing risks offshore by thoroughly reviewing each permitted activity on a case-by-case basis that is consistent with the level of risk that each activity carries.

BSEE's continued improvements in predictability and consistency in permitting are evidenced by the record number of rigs currently drilling in deepwater in the Gulf of Mexico (GOM) and the ongoing work for 8 new floating platforms in the GOM that are expected to add up to 700,000 barrels of oil per day capacity in 2014 through 2016. Additional discoveries under evaluation for development in the deepwater GOM could facilitate development of an additional 700,000 barrels of oil per day capacity by 2020. The Energy Information Administration forecasts oil production from the GOM to increase to nearly 2 million barrels per day by 2016.

Industry continues to view GOM deepwater as a major development target, and BSEE continues to heighten safety standards to address the challenges of operating in these areas. The GOM has recently seen a historic number of deepwater Mobile Offshore Drilling Units (MODUs) that are either working or are under contract preparing to start work. As a point of reference there were approximately 35 deepwater MODUs in April of 2010 (about 9 drillships and 26 semisubmersibles) and now there are 44 (26 drillships and 18 semisubmersibles) as of June 2014. New and revised deepwater rig contracts and BSEE interaction with industry on specific projects suggests that the number of deepwater MODUs in the GOM is expected to continue to increase through 2017. The number of deepwater MODUs is expected to vary within a range of 50 to 60 floating drilling rigs depending on the timing of development projects coming on line, trends in future discoveries and movement of rigs in and out of the GOM as exploration and development activities increase globally.

BSEE remains committed to its efforts to increase efficiency and transparency in its permitting process. For example, BSEE is developing an ePermitting system that should provide companies with additional information about permitting requirements, leading to increased predictability and transparency in the permitting process. The system should also allow BSEE personnel to more easily focus on proposed activities with higher risk levels, thus helping BSEE fulfill its mission of protecting both offshore workers and the environment.

Conclusion

Chair Landrieu and Members of the Committee, thank you again for inviting me to appear before your Committee. I look forward to working with the Committee especially as we proceed with development of the new Five Year Program. I am happy to answer any questions.

The CHAIR. Thank you very much.

Mr. Sieminski.

STATEMENT OF ADAM SIEMINSKI, ADMINISTRATOR, ENERGY INFORMATION ADMINISTRATION

Mr. SIEMINSKI. Chair Landrieu, I had some slides but I think we'll just do it without those. They are up here, but——

The CHAIR. Is it—we have a technical difficulty?

Mr. SIEMINSKI. No. I'm going to need somebody to——

The CHAIR. No, please. We'd love to see them if you can get somebody to help you.

Mr. SIEMINSKI. Maybe we can have a volunteer?

The CHAIR. Yes.

Pat, you want to volunteer or T Brad? Who is sitting there?

Or if you want to sit there you're welcome to.

Mr. SIEMINSKI. This will work. Maybe this is going to work.

Here we go. High tech.

The CHAIR. Go right ahead. I'm impressed.

Mr. SIEMINSKI. Chair Landrieu, it's a real pleasure. I appreciate the opportunity to be here today here in Lafayette.

The Energy Information Administration, as you know, is the independent and impartial statistical and analytical agency within the U.S. Department of Energy. My views expressed here today should not be construed as representing those of the Department of Energy or any other Federal agency. My testimony focuses on the outlook for oil and natural gas development on the Outer Continental Shelf and draws on EIA's short term energy outlook and the 2014 Annual Energy Outlook which includes long term projections out to the year 2040.

It is important to recognize that projections of energy markets are highly uncertain and subject to many unforeseeable events. The Annual Energy Outlook reference case represents an energy future based on given market, technological, demographic and other trends, current laws and regulations in consumer behavior. The complete 2014 version of the Annual Energy Outlook which we call the AEO was just released in May and it includes side cases with alternative assumptions regarding resources, technology advances and world energy prices that could significantly affect projections for oil and natural gas production.

So just as an example. This slide shows that under the high oil price scenario projected lower 48 States offshore oil production in 2040 is almost 10 percent above the reference case.

In the short term, EIA's forecast of annual average production from the Federal Gulf of Mexico increases from 1.3 million barrels a day in 2013 to 1.7 million barrels a day in 2015. At the same time due to relatively low natural gas prices the Gulf of Mexico gas production is forecast to decrease somewhat from 3.6 billion cubic feet a day to 3.2 bcf a day over the same period.

Over the longer term under the AEO 2014 reference case and that's shown here in this slide. Oil production on Federal and State waters of the Gulf of Mexico varies between 1.3 billion barrels a day and 2 million barrels a day over the period out to 2040.

Now slide four, that's this one shows natural gas production forecast to increase from about 5.2 bcf a day to 6.8 bcf a day over the same period. Toward the end of the period the pace of exploration on production activity quickens associated predominately with discoveries in the deep water and ultra deep water portions of the Gulf of Mexico.

Slide 5 shows new offshore oil production from the Alaskan North Slope partially offsetting the decline from onshore North Slope fields.

For the high oil and gas resource case we assume more resources in Alaska and the lower 48 States offshore. This reflects more favorable resolution of uncertainty surrounding undeveloped areas where there has been little or no recent exploration.

The low oil and gas resource case reflects only uncertainty around tight and shale crude oil and natural gas resources. All other resource assumptions in the high case are unchanged from the reference case.

An important aspect of the Gulf of Mexico production is the quality of the crude oil. Recent and forecast increases in domestic crude production have sparked discussion on the topic of how rising crude oil volumes will be absorbed in the U.S. refining system. U.S. crude streams vary widely in quality and the economics for U.S. refiners to use additional domestic production are directly dependent on the quality of the crude oil.

Slide 6 shows that EIA's analysis of current forecast crude production indicates that U.S. supply of lighter, API gravity crude will continue to outpace that of the medium and heavier grades. EIA expects that more than 60 percent of production growth for 2014 and 2015 will consist of sweet grades with API gravity of 40 degrees or above.

By contrast the Gulf of Mexico crudes are medium, sour with an API gravity range of 27 to 35 degrees. These crudes are particularly favored by the sophisticated world class refineries along the Gulf Coast here.

So one of the interesting things that you should see in that graph, that hatched red area to the bottom. There is some growth in there although the scale is a little hard to see. We're expecting quite a decent pick up of production of the API 27 to 35 degree crudes, most of that coming from the Gulf of Mexico in 2015. That should actually help to alleviate some of the difficulties that refiners have been having access to the heavier domestic crudes.

A key element of the survey that we have been thinking about, in fact EIA is currently working on a proposal that would expand one of our surveys that we think is going to be critical to ensuring timely and quality information on domestic oil and gas production. A key element of this survey is the inclusion of oil production by crude oil type or API gravity. We are working closely with the industry associations to ensure that this survey will be a success.

This final figure, Senator, and I'll just wrap it up then, puts the offshore production situation into the context of total national oil production.

Under EIA's reference case net oil import dependence which you see had been as high as 60 percent back in 2005 has declined very rapidly as production in onshore and offshore waters has increased.

Under EIA's reference case net oil import dependence declines 25 percent in 2016.

Under the high resource case net import dependence actually continues to decline as production rises and that's that, kind of, dotted blue line that you see there going up. At some point it is possible in the period after 2030 that the U.S. might actually be self sufficient in net oil imports.

I'd like to thank you very much for the opportunity to testify here today. As Walter said, I'd be happy to answer any questions.

[The prepared statement of Mr. Sieminski follows:]

PREPARED STATEMENT OF ADAM SIEMINSKI, ADMINISTRATOR, ENERGY INFORMATION ADMINISTRATION, DEPARTMENT OF ENERGY

Chair Landrieu and Members of the Committee, I appreciate the opportunity to appear before you today.

The Energy Information Administration (EIA) is the statistical and analytical agency within the U.S. Department of Energy. EIA collects, analyzes, and disseminates independent and impartial energy information to promote sound policymaking, efficient markets, and public understanding regarding energy and its interaction with the economy and the environment. EIA is the nation's premier source of energy information and, by law, its data, analyses, and forecasts are independent of approval by any other officer or employee of the United States Government. The views expressed herein should therefore not be construed as representing those of the Department of Energy or any other federal agency.

As requested, my testimony focuses on the outlook for oil and natural gas development on the Outer Continental Shelf (OCS). My testimony draws on EIA's June Short Term Energy Outlook (STEO) and the 2014 Annual Energy Outlook (AEO2014) which includes long-term projections through 2040. EIA released the Reference case projections for the AEO2014 in December. The Reference case is intended to represent an energy future through 2040 based on given market, technological, and demographic trends; current laws and regulations; and consumer behavior. EIA recognizes that projections of energy markets are highly uncertain and subject to geopolitical disruptions, technological breakthroughs, economic fluctuations, and other unforeseeable events. In addition, long-term trends in technology development, demographics, economic growth, and energy resources may evolve along a different path than represented in the Reference case projections.

The complete AEO2014, which was released in May, includes alternative assumptions regarding resources, technology advances, and world energy prices that can significantly affect projections for oil and natural gas production. The impact of alternative assumptions in these two areas were explored in AEO2014 side cases that address high and low oil price scenarios and more optimistic and pessimistic assumptions regarding the resource base and the pace of technology advances. The impacts of the revised assumptions in the alternative scenarios can be substantial. For example, projected offshore oil production in 2040 is roughly 10 percent above the Reference case level in the High Oil Price scenario (*Figure 1).

In the June STEO, based on forecasts of annual average production from 2013 to 2015, the federal Gulf of Mexico oil production increases from 1.3 million bbl/d to 1.7 million bbl/d. Natural gas production is forecast to decrease from 3.6 Bcf/d to 3.2 Bcf/d over the same period because natural gas prices remain low relative to oil prices.

Looking at the longer-term picture, in the AEO2014 reference case, Gulf of Mexico (federal and state) oil production varies between 1.3 million bbl/d and 2.0 million bbl/d over the projection period, 2013-2040 (Figure 2). Natural gas production in the Gulf of Mexico is forecast to increase from 1.9 Tcf (5.2 Bcf/d) to 2.5 Tcf (6.8 Bcf/d) over the same period (Figure 3). Toward the end of the period, the pace of exploration and production activity quickens, and new large development projects, associated predominantly with discoveries in the deepwater and ultra-deepwater portions of the Gulf of Mexico, are brought on stream. New offshore oil production from the Alaska North Slope partially offsets the decline in production from onshore North Slope fields, as shown in Figure 4.

For the High Oil and Gas Resource case, we assumed that there are more resources in Alaska and in the lower 48 offshore, including the development of tight oil in Alaska and 50 percent higher technically recoverable undiscovered resources for other Alaska crude oil and the lower 48 offshore (which reflects more favorable resolution of the uncertainty surrounding undeveloped areas where there has been little or no exploration and development activity, and where modern seismic survey data are lacking).

The Low Oil and Gas Resource case reflects only the uncertainty around tight and shale crude oil and natural gas resources-specifically, whether the performance of current and future wells drilled will actually be less than estimated. All other resource assumptions are unchanged from the Reference case.

Another aspect of Gulf of Mexico production that I would like to highlight relates to the quality of the crude. Recent and forecast increases in domestic crude production have sparked discussion on the topic of how rising crude oil volumes will be absorbed. EIA recently released a short-term forecast of domestic production by crude type, supplementing the May 2014 overall production forecast provided in the STEO. Forecasts of production by crude type matter for several reasons. First, U.S. crude streams vary widely in quality. Second, the economics surrounding various options for the domestic use of additional domestic oil production are directly dependent on crude quality characteristics. EIA analysis of current and forecast crude oil production indicates that U.S. supply of lighter API gravity crude will continue to outpace that of medium and heavier crudes (Figure 5). More than 60 percent of EIA's forecast of production growth for 2014 and 2015 consists of sweet grades with API gravity of 40 or above. The type of heavier crude from the OCS, in particular, the Gulf of Mexico, however, is particularly favored by refineries in the Gulf Coast. Gulf of Mexico oil production is understood to be API gravity range of 27-35 degrees, and is medium sour. Alaska crude, on and offshore, is in the same API gravity range.

I would like to mention EIA's pending proposal to expand one of our important production surveys. The quality and timeliness of well-level data on production by crude type used to develop the estimates vary widely across states. As part of its continuing effort to improve data on oil and natural gas production, EIA is now seeking public comment on a plan to expand its current collection of monthly natural gas production data in six states to include both oil and natural gas production in 19 states plus the Gulf of Mexico. The proposed data collection, which EIA plans to launch in 2015, would provide information on production by crude type. Updated estimates of regional production by crude type will also be needed as new plays start commercial development, because production from new plays will change the

---

*All figures have been retained in committee files.

14

distribution of production by crude types in the regions where those plays are located.

Finally, to put the offshore development into the national energy context, my last slide shows that under EIA's reference case, net oil import dependence declines from a high of 60 percent in 2005 to 25 percent in 2016 (Figure 6). Under the high resource case, net import dependence declines rapidly and could approach net oil self-sufficiency in the period after 2030.

The CHAIR. Thanks. I just want to make sure that last sentence was in 2030 the U.S. will be completely free of the necessity for imports?

Mr. SIEMINSKI. We would have its net imports, Senator.

The CHAIR. OK.

Mr. SIEMINSKI. So we would still be importing oil.

There are a number of places in the East Coast, the West Coast and even here along the Gulf Coast where it would still make sense to bring in a particular grade of crude oil to be run through the refineries here. But if you add all of the production up, take away the imports. We might actually have more production than we do imports on a net basis.

The CHAIR. OK, which would provide an opportunity for export either than or before depending on——

Mr. SIEMINSKI. Yes. That's exactly correct.

The CHAIR. Yes, that's what this information will help us.

Let me begin with just a few questions.

This is a little confusing to me. Maybe it will be to those listening. Your testimony currently States that we're producing 1.3 million barrels of oil a day in the OCS. In 2 years you expect it to go to 1.7 million which is a 300,000 barrel increase in 3 years.

The next paragraph says—that's the short run.

The next paragraph says in the long run which is from 2017 to 2040, you were estimating the same increase over that period of time which is 23 years as you are in the next 2. Why is that?

Are you standing on those projections?

What are some of your underlining assumptions that would make that projection so conservative?

Mr. SIEMINSKI. Senator, recent wells drilled in the Gulf of Mexico have exhibited a relatively low gas to oil ratio and that tends to keep our gas number down. The oil production itself, some of the drilling is going to have to offset natural declines that take place in the existing wells. So we may actually have more new production coming on than you get in the total number because you've got to offset the declines in the wells.

It is worth noting that the numbers that I mentioned excludes State waters. State waters would add for natural gas, for example, another 1.5.

The CHAIR. But I just want to stay for oil. Let's just talk about oil.

Mr. SIEMINSKI. Just oil.

The CHAIR. Just oil. No gas.

Mr. SIEMINSKI. Right.

The CHAIR. I just want to keep—I want to compare apples to apples.

Mr. SIEMINSKI. Then we'll just——

The CHAIR. So in your testimony, now I'm going to press this with you. In your testimony you say that in the next 2 years the amount of oil is going to increase in 2 years by 300,000 barrels a day.

Then you project that over the next 23 years it will only increase by 300,000 over that period.

That just seems—it just doesn't seem plausible.

Mr. SIEMINSKI. Our geologists look at the resource base. They look at what land is available for leasing. They look at the activity of the industry in picking up those leases. They try to make assumptions about the price of oil, the technology and so on. The numbers that they come up with suggest that it is going to be hard to grow the Gulf of Mexico oil base in the same manner that we seem to be capable of growing it onshore at this time.

So there's 2 other things that I would mention that could change. That's the technology. The increased application, just as an example of hydraulic fracturing in the offshore similar to what we're doing onshore might make those projections very different.

Another possibility and as Dr. Cruickshank mentioned, policy issues such as agreements with Mexico or even Cuba that could open up more U.S. boundary waters for development and would add to the acreage available for exploration.

The CHAIR. I'm going to actually ask the staff to draft a question to the committee. We don't have it for right now. What are the four largest investors in the Gulf of Mexico in the deep water and if they would share, if it's not proprietary, their projections of the same timeframe. What they are projecting?

Because I want to understand if there is a delta between what the government is projecting in oil production in the Gulf from the 3 to 4 major operators that have a lot of private capital to risk. We don't risk private capital. We risk other things, but not private capital, the government does.

But my indication is that the operators are feeling bullish. So I'm having a hard time understanding why they would be so bullish if there's nothing to find. I'm going to have to resolve that. I can't do that today. But it seems like a very——

The CHAIR. Then my second question and I will send in writing to you is this one.

You're projecting 23 years from 2017 forward. I want you to go back 23 years and find the government data that projected how much oil would be produced this, today, in the Gulf 23 years ago. I want to see how accurate you were then.

Because I think you're going to be wildly off. I'm trying to get to the bottom of why the government projections are so wildly off of what is the actual. I'm just seeing this decade after decade after decade.

I've got to figure out what information you all are looking at than other people are looking at. But we'll see. Maybe 23 years ago you projected that we would be generating, this very close, to the amount of oil that we're projecting. I doubt that would be the case.

I know it's difficult to, but it's not impossible. It's difficult, but not impossible to get accurate estimates because we need them. We need to know how many refineries to build. We need to know, you know, what kind of refineries to build. We need to know what kind of oil we can export. We've got to have it very accurate.

The CHAIR. The other question I wanted to ask you is on what technological basis do you decide if there's oil or gas there if you don't to seismic? Or maybe I should put it this way, what are the new technologies that the government uses either by itself of with the private sector that allow you to actually know what the resource base is? Is number one.

No. 2. Can you make an accurate projection of the resource base without testing or doing seismic? I'm going to ask the industry the same question.

Mr. SIEMINSKI. Right. On that question, Senator, I'd say that asking that of the folks at the US Geologic Survey and some of the industry people might be a good idea.

I can tell you that when EIA looks at it we try to do something similar to what other geologists do and that is look at the amount of rock that's available for production and compare that with what recovery rates have been from that resource base and use that as a methodology to project production going out into the future. It's subject to lots of problems. The main one is you have a very, very hard time dealing with changes in technology such as 3D seismic, horizontal drilling, hydraulic fracturing, stages, multi stage hydraulic fracturing and so on. All of which have tremendously boosted oil production projections, actual production and projections of those—that production in the onshore area.

The other big unknown is the price of oil and what the price of oil was at port in terms of industry activity. So we do the best that we can with the tools that we have available. I certainly wouldn't want to claim here that our reference case forecast for the year 2040 is going to be absolutely correct.

One of the things that I'll close on this comment, Senator, for this question is that that doesn't mean that reference case projections are not valuable. One of the things that you can do with a reference case projection and then you very clearly state what the assumptions are and you have those assumptions very transparent so that others can look at them and test the assumptions as you can go on side cases so we can look at a higher oil or a lower oil price case.

We can look at what better economic or worse economic case and other potential changes like that or even policy changes. When you have that reference case to run those against it leads to, I think, a little bit better view of what might be possible.

The CHAIR. But just to follow on just for a minute and then go to Mr. Cruickshank.

In the Gulf you can look at the East Gulf, the Central Gulf and the Western Gulf. You know, there have been, I think, 40,000 wells drilled in the Gulf of Mexico, roughly. But I can't remember exactly how many shallow or deep.

But I remember this from the Mercado well blew up and I had to go on the Floor and talk about how they had safely drilled about 40,000 and sometimes bad accidents will happen like that, which we hope to always avoid. But there's a lot of activity in the Gulf.

Do you know how many wells have ever been drilled in the Mid Atlantic offshore? I don't think any.

Do you know how much seismic has been done either in the South Atlantic, the Mid Atlantic or the North Atlantic?

Mr. SIEMINSKI. But I think you're right. I think it's pretty limited.

The CHAIR. Mr. Cruickshank, can you answer that question?

Mr. CRUICKSHANK. Yes, Senator.

There have been—I'm going to have to get the exact number. They have been in the order of 35 to 40 wells drilled in the Atlantic.

The CHAIR. Thirty-five and 40. There have been 40,000 in the Gulf. So just as a comparison, only 30 to 40 in the Atlantic.

How many in the Pacific? Do you know?

Mr. CRUICKSHANK. In the Pacific there's ongoing production offshore, southern California.

The CHAIR. So do we know how much out of how many wells? It's only a handful, like 20 or 30 or something like that.

Mr. CRUICKSHANK. There are 23 producing platforms.

The CHAIR. Only 23 producing platforms.

Do we know how many producing platforms we have in the Gulf?

Mr. CRUICKSHANK. I don't know the number off the top of my head. I think it's on the order of 3,000 to 3,500, something like that.

The CHAIR. It's just so important for the country just to understand the relative nature of this.

Fourty thousand wells drilled in the Gulf.

Three thousand producing platforms in the Gulf.

Twenty-five wells or so much in the whole Pacific and 23 producing platforms in the Atlantic.

There's one energy coast. That would be our coast. The others are other kinds of coast. They're not the energy coast.

So what we find in the Gulf, which is the important thing, I think, to know about is the more we look, we find. The more we drill the more resources we get. The more resources we get the richer all the people of our country become.

If it's conducted correctly it can be just a tremendously positive impact to the—I mean to the economy. You know, not harmful to the environment if it's done in the correct way.

So I'm going to be pursuing because it's very interesting to me when people say they think they know how much oil and gas is out there. I always want to say, well how would you know it?

[Laughter.]

The CHAIR. I don't know. Maybe the industry can help us figure that out.

But let me go on because we've got to move to our second panel.

Mr. Cruickshank, regarding BOEM's pursuit of scientific information about the scope and location of potential oil and gas, what is your timeframe for obtaining this information for the Mid and South Atlantic?

What steps will BOEM carry out during this timeframe?

How do you collect information about the Mid and South Atlantic, kind of following up on what we're saying because you've got to put the next 5 year plan together.

What are you looking for to try to get the information for the Mid and South Atlantic?

Mr. CRUICKSHANK. To start with there are the geologic and geophysical surveys. We expect to issue the record of decision on the programmatic EIS that we published recently. That record of decision should come out in the coming weeks.

At that point of the companies that have applied for G and G permits will be able to pursue those permits. They will need to get authorizations under the Marine Mammal Protection Act from NOAA as well as our permits. But we're hoping that by the end of the year, early 2015, the companies can be out there collecting seismic information.

That information is available to us at basically, at the cost of production as part of the terms of the permit. We will use that information in our future decisionmaking.

The CHAIR. OK.

Getting back to the Gulf of Mexico. Our operators here tell me consistently, repeatedly, that costs have gone up significantly since the Deep Water Horizon Mercando event in 2010. As you know, unnecessary regulatory costs can contribute to fewer wells being drilled, fewer royalty payments to the Federal Government which should be of some concern, as well as a decrease energy supply for the Nation.

Now appropriate regulation is always, actually, welcomed. It's a good thing. But do you have an estimate based on pre Mercando and post Mercando?

What increases have—what do you acknowledge that increase to be? What is the official understanding of the Department? Is it a 5-percent increase in drilling costs? A 10-percent? 20 percent or north of 20 or 25?

Mr. CRUICKSHANK. That is something actually that our sister agency, the Bureau of Safety and Environmental Enforcement would be more likely to know. So I like to refer the question to them and we'll get back to you.

The CHAIR. Because between the two of you all understanding what those costs are are important because that has got to be figured into your assumption whether people are going to be drilling or not. So I think it's important for both of your agencies to know that as well as for us.

We'll direct the question appropriately, but we'd ask you to get that information as well.

The CHAIR. Let me ask Mr. Sieminski this.

Regarding your assessment due to the relatively low natural gas price, gas production is forecasted to decrease in the short term. Do you believe this decreased production will increase natural gas prices in the short term?

Approximately what length of time do you mean by short term?

Do you believe that limited amounts of natural gas exports—I'll get to the export question in a minute.

Just answer those first 2 and then I'll get to exports.

Mr. SIEMINSKI. Short term for us, Senator, is the timeframe for the EIA short term Energy Outlook goes out to the end.

The CHAIR. Which is 2 years?

Mr. SIEMINSKI. Yes, 2 years.

The CHAIR. Your long term is 40?

Mr. SIEMINSKI. Twenty-five years.

The CHAIR. Twenty-five.

Mr. SIEMINSKI. Right.

The CHAIR. Do you have anything in the middle that seem? Two years to me is like two short to be of use and 25 years is like too long to count on. So I'm wondering why you don't do 8 to 12.

Mr. SIEMINSKI. The Annual Energy Outlook does include projections, you know, in annual increments all the way out to the year 2040. So you can get some medium term forecast from that. But——

The CHAIR. OK.

So what's your short term forecast?

What's your short term forecast for gas prices?

Mr. SIEMINSKI. Short term forecast is, for gas prices, to hold at around $4 a million btu.

Over the longer term we expect that to climb up over, you know, toward $6 and that is in the period out to 2030.

The CHAIR. OK, which is a long time to project. I have some issues with trying to project out that far.

But what are your assumptions about exports and what volume of exports is included in that assumption?

The CHAIR. Of gas.

Mr. SIEMINSKI. Right. For natural gas in the very short run——

The CHAIR. No. Over that longer period.

Mr. SIEMINSKI. The longer period?

The CHAIR. What are your assumptions for exports?

Mr. SIEMINSKI. Alright.

We have—that's built into the Annual Energy Outlook. We assume that there will be a couple of LNG. So I presume the exports you're talking about are not to Mexico which we actually do see pipeline exports increasing there. The possibility of some pipeline exports to Canada.

The thing that most people have been looking at very closely is LNG, liquefied natural gas exports. EIA's assumptions include a couple in the medium term. So let's say out in the next 5 years. A couple of——

The CHAIR. But the volume. It's got to be 12 to 20.

Mr. SIEMINSKI. Right. Up to——

The CHAIR. Something like that. What are you all estimating?

Mr. SIEMINSKI. We are up to a little over 10 billion cubic feet a day at the end of the timeframe.

The CHAIR. In your estimates.

Mr. SIEMINSKI. We are going to begin to do some work to look at the possibility of what it would mean if exports of LNG approach something closer to your 20 bcf a day figure.

The CHAIR. Then finally in your long term which I have difficulty accepting, but for the purposes of this discussion, your long term is that gas would be at 6. What do you have oil at the equivalent number at the same time you have gas, you know, rising to 6. What is your oil production?

Mr. SIEMINSKI. I think by 2040 we actually have natural gas prices up to just a little under $7 so we could get to 6 in around 2030.

The CHAIR. OK.

Mr. SIEMINSKI. For oil prices in the reference case continue to climb in real terms by a few percentage points per year. So that

20

by 2040 you're up to about 100 and—I think it's $140. But I'll supply that number to you for the record.

The CHAIR. One hundred dollars a barrel?

Mr. SIEMINSKI. Right.

The CHAIR. Yes, that's not going to be really good news for consumers in the country for gas. It will be very good for the producers who want to explore and make a significant profit for the exploration. But for consumers.

So gas is still going to be a bargain if we could get more of it. I would think it would really be very helpful to the country.

Mr. SIEMINSKI. You're absolutely right about that.

We see a gas price to oil ratio continuing to favor, in a sense, oil which makes natural gas attractive to both industrial users and other consumers of natural gas. Because of that in the Annual Energy Outlook we have rising use of natural gas by electric utilities, by industrial users and even in the transportation area.

The CHAIR. OK.

Do you all have any final comments you'd like to make? Thirty seconds closing each before we go to the second panel.

Mr. SIEMINSKI. One of the—your questions, Senator, had to do with, you know, finding oil.

Yes, I think it is pretty critical to drill. There are about, I think, more than 100 rigs looking for oil and gas in the Gulf of Mexico and there are no rigs drilling for oil in the Atlantic right now. The history of the oil industry is that you find more oil by drilling holes than you do with models and geologic interpretation.

Mr. CRUICKSHANK. I would just close by reiterating we look forward to working with you on the development of the next 5 year program where areas in the Atlantic and really the entire OCS is on the table for discussion right now. We'll see where that decision-making takes us.

The CHAIR. Thank you.

We don't want to leave out Alaska. Unfortunately Alaska is not on this chart. So we'll try to get something up for our next hearing because that's a very important part of the country.

Of course in Alaska people don't realize but it takes up about half of the continent of the lower 48 basically. That's how big Alaska is. It's—you have that map? Good. I thought you might have brought it.

We should put up Alaska, not to leave Alaska out. They would not be happy about that.

But they have most of the opportunities for offshore and, you know, different temperature and climate issues, particularly on the North of Alaska. South is more moderate. But we'll talk about that later with some of the other panelists.

Alright, thank you all very much. Appreciate your testimony.

If the second panel will come forward?

Thank you very much.

Our second—and as they come forward I'll introduce them for efficiency purposes.

First I'd like to welcome Mr. Kent Satterlee, III, Manager of Regulatory Policy for Offshore, Upstream America at Shell Exploration and Production Company. Shell is one of the largest lease holders and producers on the U.S. Outer Continental Shelf and a leader in Alaska production.

To be fully disclosed here, Kent is also my first cousin. I'm very proud of Kent. So thank you, Kent, for joining us.

Next we have Mr. Joe Leimkuhler, lime cooler, Vice President-Drilling of LLOG Exploration Company right here at home. I understand that Mr. Leimkuhler has over 30 years of industry experience in both onshore and offshore drilling. Currently oversees drilling at one of the top companies operating in the Gulf of Mexico.

Next we have—and please you all can be seated.

Next we have Mr. Court Ramsay, President and CEO of Aries Marine Corporation. Mr. Ramsay brings over 20 years of experience in the oil and gas marine industry. His company Aries Marine operates a diverse fleet of self evaluating—self elevating work boats and supply vessels in the Gulf of Mexico working with both major and independent producers.

We have Mr. Oneil Malbrough, Executive Director of Coastal Ports and Marine Environment and Infrastructure of CB and I, one of the world's largest energy infrastructure companies with a large presence in the Gulf of Mexico and a significant corporate presence in Baton Rouge, Louisiana. We welcome you.

Finally Mr. Chett Chiasson, Executive Director of Port Fourchon. As we all know Port Fourchon provides vital supplies and services to the Gulf of Mexico offshore, deep water oil platforms. It's truly a phenomenal and essential energy port that does it all for the deep water. We look forward to hearing from your comments, particularly about the infrastructure challenges that affect our 5 year oil and gas plan for the Nation.

So Mr. Satterlee, we will begin with you.

We ask you all to limit your remarks to 5 minutes as time allows we'll have you be able to add. Of course, you can fill in some of the things if you didn't get to say it in your time in questions. We thank you very much.

You may have to lean into the microphone.

Thank you very much for the work that Shell does and for your extraordinary commitment to this area, post Katrina and Mercando.

STATEMENT OF KENT SATTERLEE, MANAGER, OFFSHORE REGULATORY POLICY, SHELL EXPLORATION AND PRODUCTION COMPANY

Mr. SATTERLEE. Thank you, Madame Chair. Thank you for the opportunity to testify today on behalf of Shell to examine OCS production and what it means for our country. This hearing is timely as both the Federal and State governments work to address energy supply and demand, climate challenges and continued economic recovery.

We live in a world facing significant increases in demand globally. In order to meet the growing global energy demand the U.S. needs access to more domestic oil and gas because we can't continue to depend on foreign supplies when most of the expected population growth is in other countries that are competing with the U.S. for energy. The OCS offers a bountiful resource, much of which is untapped.

U.S. domestic oil and gas production is up. That's good news because energy from coal resources is down and renewable energy, like wind and solar, is not expected to increase appreciably according to the EIA. We have witnessed the greatest energy expansion in the history of the world with our U.S. onshore, unconventional gas. We have the ability to see a similar expansion in supply from the offshore.

In 2013 the Gulf of Mexico produced 457 million barrels of oil in condensate down from a record OCS oil production of 570 million barrels in 2009. Natural gas production in the Gulf of Mexico is also down from a high of 5 trillion cubic feet in 2000 to just above one tcf in 2013. We can do better.

The BOEM estimates 88.6 billion barrels of oil and 398.4 trillion cubic feet of gas have yet to be discovered on the U.S. OCS. A significant amount of those resources are located in the Eastern Gulf of Mexico and in the Atlantic where they remain off limits to oil and gas exploration and development. According to the BOEM, 87 percent of offshore acreage is off limits.

A 2011 study by Wood Mackenzie shows that developing these off limit areas could create more than one million new jobs and generate $127 billion in new government revenue by the year 2020.

Energy producers, including Shell, carefully evaluate when, how and where they will invest in opportunities globally. As you can see from the gap on the map, our neighbors to the north and the south, moving forward developing their oil and gas resources where safety, environmental protection and jobs and revenue are equally important. With offshore access growing across Canada, Mexico and Latin America, the U.S. risks losing jobs, revenue and technology to other countries if we continue to block further development. Competition for investments in recent and upcoming bid rounds will widen this development gap.

Since Mercando the root cause cementing issues have been addressed and a new industry standard. Other new and revised standards address deep water wall construction, operator and contractor management systems and blow out prevention equipment. But we are confident that we can drill and produce safely at deep water locations in the Gulf and elsewhere on the OCS. Continuous improvement is our goal. We can never be satisfied.

We need to act now though. We can start in 4 key areas.

No. 1, include today's off limit lease areas in the next 5 year plan so we can access and explore these significant opportunities, particularly in the Eastern Gulf of Mexico and in the Mid and South Atlantic margin.

In order to have new OCS access available for leasing during this period it is crucial that Interior include these areas in a Section 18 review and in their EIS. It must also move quickly to approve seismic permits so that new resource data can be collected. Seismic acquisition properly mitigated causes no harm to marine animals.

No. 2, enact Federal revenue sharing legislation which allocates bonus and royalty revenues to the those coastal States with existing or planned offshore development. As you have already done for the Gulf of Mexico and are seeking to expand.

No. 3, adopt performance based regulatory oversight programs.

The U.S. must improve the efficiency of its regulatory system. As our regulatory regime continues to evolve we urge you to work with Federal regulators to achieve regulatory certainty for our industry. Permits to explore and develop must be reasonable and issued expeditiously.

For example, over a year for an air permit from EPA to drilling exploratory well in the Eastern Gulf of Mexico is not reasonable.

Fourthly, recognize the benefits of America's oil and gas resources and the opportunities that it brings all Americans, not just those who work in our industry.

To achieve this our Federal Government must enact policies that encourage investment here in the U.S.

The U.S. could sit on the sidelines and watch as neighboring countries explore offshore opportunities or we can work together toward a common goal safely, responsibly and efficiently harnessing the benefits of our resources for our country, for America's energy future.

Thank you very much.

[The prepared statement of Mr. Satterlee follows:]

PREPARED STATEMENT OF KENT SATTERLEE, MANAGER, OFFSHORE REGULATORY POLICY, SHELL EXPLORATION AND PRODUCTION COMPANY

Madame Chair and members of the Committee, thank you for the opportunity to testify today of behalf of Shell Oil Company at this hearing to examine Outer Continental Shelf (OCS) production and why it is important for our country.

This hearing is timely as both the federal and state governments work to address energy supply and demand, climate challenges, and continued economic recovery.

Shell is an integrated oil and gas company, dedicated to meeting ever-growing energy demands efficiently and responsibly. We are active in more than 70 countries, and have a long history of deepwater development. At Shell, safety, sustainability, innovative technologies, and new, viable energy sources are essential. They are our business.

We live in a world facing significant increases in demand globally. The US Census Bureau puts the world population at over 7 billion today and estimates it to reach 8 billion by 2025 and 9 billion by 2040. Energy consumption to provide for the needs of these people is expected to increase 56 percent by 2040. In order to meet growing, global energy demand, the U.S. needs access to more domestic oil and gas because we can't continue to depend on foreign supplies when most of the expected population growth is in other countries that are competing with the U.S. for energy. The OCS offers a bountiful resource, much of which is untapped.

U.S. domestic oil and gas production is up. That's good news, because energy from coal resources is down; and renewable energy, like wind and solar, is not expected to increase appreciably, according to the EIA. We have witnessed the greatest energy expansion in the history of the world with our U.S. onshore unconventional gas, and we have the ability to see a similar expansion in supply from the offshore. The Bureau of Ocean Exploration and Management (BOEM) estimates 88.6 billion barrels of oil and 398.4 trillion cubic feet of gas have yet to be discovered on the U.S. OCS. In 2013, the Gulf of Mexico produced 457 million barrels of oil and condensate, down from a record OCS oil production of 570 million in 2009. Natural gas production in the Gulf of Mexico is also down from a high of 5 trillion cubic feet in 2000 to just above 1 TCF in 2013.

And a significant amount of those resources are located in the eastern Gulf of Mexico and in the Atlantic-where they remain "off limits" to oil and gas exploration and development. According to the BOEM, 87 percent of offshore acreage is "off limits".

A 2011 study by Wood Mackenzie shows that developing these "off limit areas" could:

• Create more than 1 million new jobs; and
• Generate $127 billion in new government revenue by 2020.

According to Interior's analyses, conducted pursuant to Section 18 of the OCS Lands Act, it is estimated that over $1 trillion in net economic value is associated with development of the GOM over the past 20 years. Studies of employment benefits estimate that over 150,000 direct jobs are associated with GOM federal offshore development. In addition, there are "multiplier" effects which extend to virtually all of the 50 states. The Federal government has collected over a $150 billion in revenues.

While official DOI resource assessments in the 1980's heavily discounted any possibility of significant resource potential in the deepwater GOM, exploration results proved otherwise. Our industry has continued to find new reserves and has successfully developed the technology to recover them. Energy producers, including Shell, carefully evaluate when, how and where they invest in opportunities globally.

As you can see from the gap on the map, our neighbors to the north and south are moving forward, developing their oil and gas resources—where safety, environmental protection, jobs and revenue are equally important. With offshore access growing across Canada, Mexico and Latin America, the U.S. risks losing jobs, revenue and technology to other countries if we continue to block development. Competition for investments in recent and upcoming bid rounds will widen this development gap.

Shell's experience in the Gulf of Mexico and elsewhere around the world shows that we can produce oil and gas safely and efficiently, and our technology is helping us produce more with a smaller environmental footprint. In the Gulf of Mexico, Shell currently operates seven major floating offshore facilities, 12 fixed structure platforms, numerous subsea production systems; and we have under contract one of the largest drilling rig fleets.

Shell urges you to support the 5-year planning process and the unanimous inclusion of all of the "off limit" lease areas, so we can access and explore these significant opportunities. Our interest is in all areas currently open for leasing in the Gulf of Mexico and offshore Alaska, but also exploration in new areas where the true potential of the resource is unknown, particularly in the Mid- and South-Atlantic as well as the Eastern Gulf of Mexico.

We can safely, responsibly and effectively harness the economic benefits of our domestic oil and gas resources for our country's gain. Shell, and the industry, recognizes the need to explore for and produce natural resources in a safe and environmentally sound manner. Post-Macondo, we all worked together— operators, regulators, government officials, community members and others to further improve and move forward to deliver much needed energy from the Gulf of Mexico.

We have seen safety standards implemented and we've seen step-changes in prevention, intervention and response—thanks to advances in technologies and utilization-all contributing to improved safety of offshore exploration. In the weeks and months following the incident, new government regulations were put in place. New and revised industry standards were developed. Also, the Marine Well Containment Company is up and running. Shell was a founding member of this industry consortium that developed and maintains a containment system for underwater well-control responses. The Center for Offshore Safety, which helps companies thoroughly and objectively audit safety and environmental management systems, is in full operation. And perhaps the most recent example of partnering, innovating and utilizing technology is Marine Vibroseis, where Total, Exxon and Shell are working together to use low frequency vibration technology to minimize underwater noise during seismic surveys. Shell is proud to have been involved in all of these game-changing initiatives.

Deepwater development has been remarkably successful, not only from an energy production standpoint, but also from a safety standpoint. For the past 18 years, the MMS (now BSEE) has required Deepwater Operations Plans (DWOPs). The DWOP process is a flexible, goal-setting regulatory approach that has facilitated deepwater development and enhanced safety. DWOPs assess risks, barriers, and operational controls for all deepwater projects. Through 2013, 1271 DWOPs had been approved for 410 projects. 5.2 billion barrels of oil and condensate and 17 tcf have been produced from these projects without a major safety incident.

Since Macondo, the root cause cementing issues have been addressed in a new industry regulatory standard. Other new or revised standards address deepwater well construction, operator and contractor management systems, and blowout prevention equipment. BSEE participates in the standards committees. While we are confident that we can drill and produce safely at deepwater locations in the Gulf and elsewhere on the OCS, continuous improvement is our goal and we can never be satisfied.

We need to act now, and we can start in 4 key areas:

1) Include—today's "off limit" lease areas in the next 5-year plan, so we can access and explore these significant opportunities, particularly in the Eastern

Gulf of Mexico and the Mid-and Southern Atlantic margin. The Interior Department has just initiated its 2017-2022 leasing plan and is accepting public comments. In order to have new OCS areas available for leasing during this period, it is crucial that Interior include these areas in its Section 18 review and EIS. It must also move to quickly approve seismic permits so that new resource data can be collected. Seismic acquisition, properly mitigated, causes no harm to marine animals.

2) Enact—Federal Revenue Sharing legislation which allocates bonus and royalty revenues to those coastal states with existing or planned offshore development, as you have already done in the Gulf of Mexico and are seeking to expand.

3) Adopt—performance-based regulatory oversight programs. The U.S. must improve the efficiency of the regulatory system. Federal agencies need to work together and be adequately funded. As our regulatory regime continues to evolve, we urge you to work with Federal regulators to achieve regulatory certainty for our industry. Permits to explore and develop must be reasonable and issued expeditiously. For example, over a year for an air permit from EPA to drill an exploratory well in the Eastern Gulf is not reasonable. With performance-based regulation and a productive collaboration between government, industry and other stakeholders, we can address concerns and move forward. We must gather the necessary science that shows that offshore development can proceed without compromising our environment. Our regulatory system has not kept pace with the technological advancements of ultra-deep water and frontier areas, like the Arctic. The U.S. has not kept pace with other countries in moving toward performance-based systems and risks falling behind.

4) Recognize—the benefits of America's oil and gas resources and the opportunities it brings to all Americans, not just those that work in our industry. The jobs created extend to most every sector of our economy, and affordable energy enables us live comfortably and invest in our economy. To achieve this, our Federal government must enact policies that encourage investment here in the U.S. and not export it to other countries.

Producing more oil and gas in our own country is a "win-win" proposition. It provides real economic and security benefits. With increased domestic production, less money is exported from the U.S., more money is invested here and federal revenues increase through royalties and taxes. This can be done in a way that provides appropriate environmental protections based on solid science.

The U.S. could sit on the sidelines, and watch as neighboring countries explore offshore opportunities, or we can work together, toward a common goal of safely, responsibly and efficiently harnessing the benefits of our resources for our country-for America's energy future.

The CHAIR. Thank you very much, Mr. Satterlee.
Mr. Leimkuhler.

STATEMENT OF JOSEPH LEIMKUHLER, VICE PRESIDENT-DRILLING, LLOG EXPLORATION COMPANY, L.L.C.

Mr. LEIMKUHLER. I also have some slides to cover so let me just put these windows up.

Madame Chair, thank you for inviting me to testify today on behalf of LLOG Exploration Company. LLOG welcomes this opportunity to provide what we see as the opportunities and challenges to further development of the Nation's resource in the Outer Continental Shelf. My goal is to provide you with a snapshot of our current operations, how those operations are conducted within the regulatory processes and what we see as improvement areas.

First, a little overview of LLOG.

I won't go over all of our history. I'll leave it there for you to look at. Unlike a super, major, LLOG being an independent we are the largest, privately owned oil producer in the OCS. As a private company, unlike a super, major, we target our areas in specific niches within the Gulf of Mexico. So the expertise and capability bring to the areas we target is indeed state-of-the-art.

I'll leave you with two main points on our background.

Safety.

At LLOG, safety is a core value. Priorities may change, but safety does not. In recognition of that value is LLOG being awarded the SOAR Award for Safe Operations and Accurate Reporting in 2008, the last year the award was made.

In terms of scope, we have 16 deep water developments to date with 8 fields in the OCS currently under development.

The core work for us centers around subsidy developments tied into floating offshore, deepwater platforms. We are the only private company to utilize this tool in the world. We use standardized well designs and standardized platform designs to be able to respond quickly to take advantage of the opportunities that the OCS provides.

We have never drilled an expendable well.

If we find oil in commercial quantities we have always found a way to produce it. We design our wells to production quality specifications so we can quickly turn our discoveries to producers as efficiently as any operator in the OCS.

However, we operate within the same leasing framework. I'm not going to go over all of these processes. I only have 5 minutes.

But I did want to point out some areas specifically where LLOG feels that improvements can be made to help us improve our operations in the Gulf of Mexico. As Kent Satterlee mentioned first of the air permits required. The Clean Air Act actually divides the jurisdiction of air permits in the Gulf of Mexico into two regions. They are not aligned with the leasing planning areas of the Gulf of Mexico.

So the first request from LLOG is that if we could have the planning for the air permits lined with at least the operating areas. Our preference would be to have BOEM manage all air permit approval for all drilling operations and production operations in the OCS. But in light of that it would be a big help to at least get it lined up with the planning areas.

As you can see in the western central—eastern central Gulf of Mexico, the EPA jurisdiction out of Atlanta and Kent already mentioned that takes a year to get that permit. The permit is also rig specific. So you have to know what rig you're going to have to contract a year in advance.

The CHAIR. That doesn't make any sense.

Mr. LEIMKUHLER. So we are applying for those permits. We're moving forward to develop the leases that LLOG has in that area, but it would make a lot more sense and be more efficient for us. We feel it can be done with no impact to compliance with the Clean Air Act.

The second issue that we find is dealing with our—with the actual capability of the regulatory agencies to process and permit our approvals. I've worked my entire career offshore since 1987 in the deep water Gulf of Mexico and the technical professionals and regional management at the MMS, what was the MMS, BOEM and BSEE that I have worked with over that time were and are consistently professional, capable and dedicated. We just need more of them.

We continue to receive our well related permits, drilling, as well as completion just in time. This is not due to a lack of effort by the BSEE and BOEM staff, but rather an understaffed situation despite the best efforts of BSEE and BOEM district and regional management to obtain and recruit talent. The overall approval cycle could be improved with increase in agency capability.

We're finding that the more knowledgeable staff are retiring which leaves the current staff shorthanded and overworked. Not to mention the lack of experience among the understaffed. This is part of the larger big crew change. It's a challenge not only for industry, but also BSEE's district managers and BOEM's regional supervisors. Because of the situation permits are being approved with a short window prior to commencement of operations which makes it difficult for us to conduct operations that require long lead time for planning and sequential approvals.

So in conclusion of this statement, additional capable agency staff equals additional permit approvals, additional production revenue and additional economic development.

Third is the comingling approval process. LLOG strives to make all the wells we drill commercial by using smart well technology to open up multiple zones and adjacent surface reservoirs within the same well.

To make our project economically viable we normally request to comingle our down hole production from these zones. Our deep water rigs often drill development wells in subsea fields where the completion of the well immediately follows the drilling process. As long as Mother Nature cooperates and we find the reservoirs in the expected locations and depths we can file for our comingling approvals in plenty of time.

However, we often find our zones do not come in as expected. We need to either file for an initial comingling permit or modify an existing permit. With a rig on location consuming over a million dollars a day in capital we need to evaluate the ability and likelihood to obtain a comingling permit approval verses the potential impact of costly delays to project profitability. Under such conditions even the expectation of delays make some zones uneconomic and thus reserves are being lost.

Additional improvement opportunities related to operations are in the areas of containment response and the impact of rigid application of the Jones Act to offshore facility installation. In containment response those needs are met by two providers, the Marine Well Containment Corporation and the Helix Well Containment Group. Both are very capable organizations that together provide a diversity of suppliers, operator expertise and response capabilities. This diversity of response should be encouraged and continued.

However, in LLOG's view this response capability is at risk of being compromised if responder immunity is not improved. We urge the passage of the proposed amendment covering improved responder immunity.

With respect to heavy lifts associated with offshore facility installations in the Jones Act, LLOG encourages the Coast Guard and regulatory agencies to adhere to the historical application of the law with respect to transport vessels. Current rigid application of the Jones Act to heavy lift vessels for the minimal distances that those vessels move the suspended load for offshore installation has resulted in increased lift complexity, scope and added risk.

In addition, LLOG feels that continued application of the Jones Act to heavy lift vessels has the potential to transfer the work away from Gulf Coast Fabrication yards.

With regard to the management of Plug and Abandonment liabilities, it is LLOG's understanding that revisions to the supplemental bonding requirements are to be released in an upcoming notice to leasees or NTO. LLOG requests that serious consideration be given to the scope of the proposed changes. If the changes are more than a refinement or clarification of the existing regulations than the rulemaking process should be followed.

Finally with regard to the regulators and operator interface we would like the Department of Interior to perform an after action review of the allocation of work scope between BOEM and BSEE. LLOG understands and supports the split of the revenue function to BOEM and the operational enforcement rule to BSEE. However in LLOG's view the full permitting and plan approval function, after the lease sale, through the full operational cycle should fall to BSEE.

Thank you for the opportunity to present the views of LLOG and myself on these issues. Safe, efficient production and use of our Nation's resources on the OCS is good for LLOG, good for Louisiana, good for Gulf Coast and good for the Nation.

[The prepared statement of Mr. Leimkuhler follows:]

PREPARED STATEMENT OF JOSEPH LEIMKUHLER, VICE PRESIDENT-DRILLING, LLOG EXPLORATION COMPANY, LLC

Madame Chair and members of the Committee, thank you for inviting me to testify today on behalf LLOG Exploration Company. LLOG welcomes this opportunity to provide what we see as the opportunities and challenges to further development of the nation's resources in the Outer Continental Shelf (OCS). My goal is to provide you a snapshot of LLOG's current operations, how those operations are conducted within the regulatory processes of the Gulf of Mexico, and what we see as improvement opportunities.

LLOG is one of the largest privately owned oil & gas firms in the country and is the largest private oil producer in the offshore US OCS. Our focus is the US Gulf of Mexico where we apply a targeted approach using floating production systems and subsea wells to safely and efficiently develop the nation's deepwater oil and gas resources.

Unlike a Super Major our areas of focus is quite limited, however the level of expertise and capability we bring to those areas is state of the art. I'll leave the LLOG company background info on this slide for your reference, but wish to highlight two main points:

Safety—At LLOG we hold safety as a core value—priorities may change but values do not. Recognition of that value is LLOG being awarded the SOAR award in 2008.

Scope—we have 16 deepwater developments to date with 8 fields in the OCS currently under development.

The core work for LLOG is the exploration of our leases in the Gulf of Mexico (GOM) utilizing standardized well designs to efficiently explore, followed by field development utilizing subsea production flowline systems that flow back to a central floating production platform. Utilizing these tools LLOG is able to construct viable economic subsea projects from multiple discoveries safely and efficiently. In our history we have yet to drill an "expendable well"—if the oil and gas are present in commercial quantities we have been able to eventually produce the well. LLOG designs our wells to production quality specifications such that we can turn our discoveries to producers safely and efficiently as any operator in the OCS.

How that process plays out within the regulatory framework is shown using a Simplified Permit Process Overview for a Subsea Well Tie in. Depending on where a subsea well is drilled in the GOM from 9-11 permits or plan approvals are needed to move a prospect from leasingto production. Those permits and plan approvals are split between BOEM (red text) and BSEE (blue text) and for the eastern Statement of Joseph Leimkuhler Vice—President—Drilling LLOG Exploration Company LLC to the U.S. Senate Committee on Energy and Natural Resources Monday, July 7, 2014 July 5th, 2014 2 portion of the central gulf planning area the EPA (bold black text). I do not have time to cover all these approvals but wish to highlight three where LLOG feels there are improvement opportunities and address other issues not indicated on this process diagram.

First is the air permits required to be compliant with the Clean Air Act (CAA). [Show Slide 6] For wells drilled in the OCS in the Western Planning area the CAA compliance is incorporated into the Exploration Plan approval process required by BOEM. This also applies to the majority of wells drilled in the Central GOM Planning Area with the exception of the Eastern portion of the Central Planning Area where EPA jurisdiction applies. The EPA air permit approval process and protocol is quite different from the BOEM protocol and takes from 12-18 months to secure. This EPA permit is actually individual rig specific versus rig type specific in the BOEM protocol and in our view adds operational complexity and delays with no actual benefit relative to CAA compliance. LLOG urges you to allow BOEM to assume CAA compliance across the GOM and at a minimum allow BOEM to administer CAA compliance for the western and central planning areas.

Second is the APD or drilling permit approval process. I have worked my entire offshore career since 1987 in the Deepwater Gulf of Mexico and the technical professionals and Regional Management at the MMS, BOEM and BSEE that I have worked with over that time were and are consistently professional, capable and dedicated . . . we just need more of them.

We continue to receive our well related permits (drilling and well as completion and workover) just in time. This is not due to a lack of effort by the BSEE and BOEM staff, but rather an understaffed situation, despite the best efforts of BSEE and BOEM district and regional management to retain and recruit talent. The overall approval cycle could be improved with an increase in agency capability.

- We are finding that the more knowledgeable staff are retiring which leaves the current staff short-handed, and overworked, not to mention the lack of experience among the younger staff. This is part of the larger "Big Crew Change" and is a challenge not only for industry but also for BSEE's District Managers and BOEM's Regional Supervisors. Because of this situation, permits are being approved with a short window prior to commencement of operations, which makes it difficult for operators to conduct operations that require a long lead time for planning and sequential approvals.

- In our opinion funding should not be an issue. Given the amount of fees charged for permitting we feel the financial resources are available. This year alone, LLOG has paid $431,507 to date in permit fees for DOCDs, EPs, APDs, APMs, Pipeline, Facility permits and rig inspection fees. With our current anticipated workload, LLOG will spend close to $1MM this year in permitting fees. This does not include the revenues paid to the federal agencies from Lease Sales, Bonuses, nor revenue from Royalties. Can this revenue stream be focused on staff retention, recruiting and capabilities within the agencies?

Additional capable agency staff=additional permit approvals, additional production revenue & additional economic development.

Third is the comingling approval process. LLOG strives to make all the wells we drill commercial by utilizing smart well technology to open up multiple zones in adjacent subsurface reservoirs within the same well. To make such projects economically viable we normally request to comingle dowhhole the production form those zones. Our deepwater rigs often drill development wells in subsea fields where the completion and subsequent production from the wells immediately follows the drilling and casing of the well in a continuous operation. As long as mother nature cooperates and we find the reservoirs in the expected location and depth, we can file for our commingling permit with plenty of time for approval. However, we often find zones that do not come in as expected and we need to either file for an initial commingling permit or modify an existing permit. With a rig on location consuming over $1 million a day in capital we need to evaluate the ability and likelihood to obtain comingling permit approval versus the impact of costly delays to the project profitability. Under such conditions even the expectation of delays makes some zones un-economic, thus reserves are being lost.

Additional improvement opportunities related to operations are in the areas of Containment Response and the impact of rigid application of the Jones Act to off-shore facility installation.

In containment response those needs are met by two providers the Marine Well Containment Corporation or MWCC and the Helix Well Containment Group (HWCG). Both are very capable organizations that together provide a diversity of suppliers, operator expertise, and response capabilities—this diversity of response should be encouraged and continued. However, in LLOG's view this response capability is at risk of being compromised if Responder Immunity is not improved. We urge the passage of the proposed amendment covering improved Responder Immunity.

With respect to heavy lifts associated with offshore facilities installations and the Jones Act. LLOG encourages the USCG and regulatory agencies to adhere to the historical application of the law with respect to transport vessels. Current rigid application of the Jones Act to heavy lift vessels for the minimal distances that these vessels move the suspended load (in most cases hundreds of feet or less) is resulting in increased lift complexity and scope and adding risk. In addition LLOG feels continued application of the Jones Act to heavy lift vessels has the potential to transfer work away from Gulf Coast Fabrication yards.

With regard to the management of Plug and Abandonment liabilities—it is LLOG's understanding that revisions to the supplemental bonding requirements are to be released in an upcoming Notice to Lessee or NTL. LLOG requests that serious consideration be given to the scope of the proposed changes. If the changes are more than a refinement or clarification of the existing regulations then the rule making process should be followed.

Finally with regard to the Regulators and Operator Interface—we would like the Dept. of Interior to perform a AAR—an After Action Review—of the allocation of work scope between BOEM and BSEE. LLOG understands and supports the split of the revenue function to BOEM and the operational enforcement role to BSEE. However, in LLOG's view the full permitting and plan approval function after the lease sale through the full operational cycle should fall to BSEE.

Thank you for the opportunity to present the views of LLOG and myself on these issues. Safe, efficient production and use of our nation's resources from the OCS is good for LLOG, Louisiana, the Gulf Coast and the Nation.

The CHAIR. Thank you very much.

Mr. Ramsay.

STATEMENT OF COURT RAMSAY, PRESIDENT, ARIES MARINE CORPORATION

Mr. RAMSAY. Good afternoon.

Thank you, Madame Chair, for the opportunity to participate in today's hearing on OCS production. My name is Court Ramsay. I'm the President of Aries Marine Corporation, an offshore marine service company here in Lafayette.

Aries Marine was founded in 1981, employs over 300 people and operates a fleet of 24 vessels.

Fifteen are self elevating work platforms, known as lift boats or jack ups and they're used in platform maintenance and repair.

The other 9 vessels are supply boats that deliver the various equipment, drilling mud and commodities to the drilling platforms.

Aries, in addition, has another 5 boats under construction, 4 of which are being built here in Louisiana.

Our fleet is part of a robust offshore support vessel industry that was born in South Louisiana and currently includes approximately 1800 work boats flying the U.S. flag. The vessels support the entire life cycle of an offshore oil and gas well. From the beginning in seismic work all the way to the end of decommissioning and plug and abandonment, the work boats are part of this valid and necessary infrastructure.

We're in the middle of a boat building boom. The energy renaissance in North America has kick started the largest ship building boom in over 3 decades. Seven hundred and fourty-five vessels are currently on order, under construction or have been recently delivered in the United States.

Some of those are product carriers.

Some of those are also offshore work boats.

Those product carriers would be hauling crude and fine crude to regions outside the Gulf Coast and the shipyards will be building OSVs to the tune of 111 contracted since 2013. We're actually a net exporter of offshore support vessels currently.

The Gulf of Mexico outlook is great. Interest in the U.S. Gulf has continued to strengthen over the last several years, especially in the deep water. There is an increase year after year of rigs working on our OCS.

The Department of Interior also held a lease sale in March for 329 Gulf tracks that brought in over $872 million in high bids.

The impact on Louisiana.

The growth in shipbuilding and the offshore exploration and production is particularly beneficial to our State. It not only employs the people in the energy sector, but it also leads the Nation in domestic maritime jobs and ranks third in shipbuilding jobs.

Some new frontiers.

Opportunities to open additional areas in Alaska and the Mid Atlantic to offshore development of fossil fuels could spur significant job growth and economic activity as will wind projects off the coast of Massachusetts, Rhode Island, Delaware, Maryland, Virginia. In order to take advantage of these opportunities though, it's imperative that the Department of Interior move forward with planned lease sales and expedite the applications for drilling permits.

Some challenges.

Despite the growth of the offshore marine industry a deluge of regulatory requirements from Washington is threatening that growth. Domestic offshore vessel companies have become collateral damage in the aftermath of the Deep Water Horizon incident and are subject to multiple overlapping and duplicative safety and environmental regimes and regulations.

One example.

Just last year the Coast Guard announced plans to require all vessels operating on the OCS to implement vessel specific safety environmental management systems, also known as SEMS plans. But vessel operators already comply with safety management and systems mandated by another Federal agency, the Bureau of Safety Environmental Enforcement. Our customers, the operators, are required to ensure that all contractors have safety policies and procedures in place to support the implementation of the operator safety management system.

Believe me, there are regular and consistent contractor audits undertaken to ensure that the contractors are in compliance with the operator's plans. This new proposed Coast Guard regulation will create 2 different safety plans for a single OCS operation by two different regulatory agencies. This makes this proposal not only duplicative, but potentially contradictory and dangerous.

Training requirements continue to rise. Our industry is also the subject of increase and then sometimes excessive training requirements for the crew members which cost the boat operators significant amounts of time and money and represent a real barrier to recruitment.

The overall impact of regulations.

The offshore marine industry believes strongly in promoting a culture of safety and environmental stewardship and instills those values on each and every one of our crew members. For years now the U.S. work boat industry has had a stellar safety record, but OSVs operating in the Gulf of Mexico today travel with bookshelves that are continuously loaded down with additional rows of plans, procedures, manuals required by multiple Federal agencies. They are continuing to overlap regulation upon regulation in the offshore environment. This trend not only makes compliance costly and difficult, it threatens to put family owned boat companies out of business and shift the focus toward paperwork instead of safe operations.

The CHAIR. Thirty seconds.

30 seconds, if you can try to wrap up.

Mr. RAMSAY. In closing I'll give you some information about my company that I'm especially proud of.

We have a loyal and dedicated work force of some of the greatest Americans alive. Over 300 employees work for Aries Marine and enjoy salaries that can support a family along with rich benefits, medical insurance, supplemental insurance and 401K retirement plans. It's a great package in any industry.

But the phenomenal thing is we provide the family's medical benefits too. Through Aries Marine over 900 people enjoy the comforts of medical insurance. That's what this industry does for America in this region. That's what this industry can do for America and other regions.

Thank you for this opportunity. I'd be happy to answer any questions you have.

[The prepared statement of Mr. Ramsay follows:]

PREPARED STATEMENT OF COURT RAMSAY, PRESIDENT, ARIES MARINE CORPORATION

Introduction

Thank you, Madam Chair, for the opportunity to participate in today's hearing on OCS production.

My name is Court Ramsay, and I am the President of Aries Marine Corporation, an offshore marine service company headquartered in Lafayette. Aries Marine was founded in 1981, employs over 300 people, and operates a fleet of 24 vessels. 15 of those are self-elevating work platforms, also known as liftboats or jackups, which are used for platform maintenance and repair, workover operations, pipeline repairs, well hookups, rig tending, and salvage operations. The other 9 vessels are supply boats that deliver equipment, drilling mud, and other commodities to offshore drilling and production operations in both shallow and deep water. Aries has another 5 boats on order right now, and has performed work for every major and most of the independent oil and gas companies in the Gulf of Mexico, as well as on the west coast, Alaska, and Hawaii.

The Aries Marine fleet is part of a robust offshore support vessel industry that was born in South Louisiana and currently includes approximately 1,800 workboats flying the U.S. flag. These vessels support the entire life cycle of an offshore oil and gas well—conducting seismic surveys, drilling test wells, towing and installing production platforms, laying pipelines, providing dive support, transporting workers, fuel, and equipment, and facilitating the decommissioning of platforms and the plugging and abandonment of wells. America's offshore workboat fleet is a critical

33

part of this nation's energy infrastructure, and we are proud as a company and an industry to support the development of natural resources in the Gulf of Mexico and elsewhere.

Opportunities

Boatbuilding Boom

The energy renaissance in North America has kick-started the largest shipbuilding boom in over three decades. 745 vessels are currently on order, under construction, or have been recently delivered in the United States. That includes 17 large product tankers and 8 coastal tank barges. In addition to those, 336 inland tank barges were delivered last year, breaking the previous record of 261 established in 2012. These vessels will facilitate increased shipping of traditional heavy and non-traditional light, sweet crude to refineries outside the Gulf region. In addition to product carriers, U.S. shipyards are also building more offshore support vessels, entering into 111 contracts in 2013 for new builds. The United States is now a net exporter of offshore support vessels as the industry tallied half a billion dollars in export revenues just last year.

Gulf of Mexico Outlook

Interest in the U.S. Gulf has continued to strengthen over the last several years, especially in deepwater. There are now 36 active rigs in the Gulf, up from 33 last year, and the Department of Interior held a lease sale in March for 329 Gulf tracts that brought in over $872 million in high bids.

Impact on Louisiana

The growth in shipbuilding and offshore exploration and production is particularly beneficial to Louisiana, which not only employs people in the energy sector, but also leads the nation in domestic maritime jobs and ranks third in shipbuilding jobs. Many of the product carriers and offshore support vessels that I mentioned are being built in Louisiana yards, by Louisiana workers, and a big chunk of those OSVs will eventually be delivered to Louisiana operators, and crewed by Louisiana mariners.

New Frontiers

Opportunities to open additional areas in Alaska and the mid-Atlantic to offshore development of fossil fuels could spur significant job growth and economic activity, as will wind projects off the coast of Massachusetts, Rhode Island, Delaware, Maryland, and Virginia. In order to take advantage of these opportunities though, it's imperative that the Department of Interior move forward with planned lease sales and expedite applications for drilling permits.

Challenges

Regulatory Environment

Despite robust growth in the offshore marine industry and opportunity on the horizon, the deluge of regulatory requirements from Washington is threatening that growth. Domestic offshore vessel companies have become collateral damage in the aftermath of the DEEPWATER HORIZON incident and the subject of multiple, overlapping, and duplicative safety and environmental regimes and regulations.

SEMS

For example, late last year the Coast Guard announced plans to require all vessels operating on the OCS to implement vessel-specific Safety and Environmental Management Systems (also known as SEMS) plans. But vessel operators already comply with Safety Management Systems mandated by another federal agency, the Bureau of Safety and Environmental Enforcement (BSEE), for all OCS lessees and their vessel contractors. Operators are required to ensure that all contractors and sub-contractors have safety policies and procedures in place that support the implementation of the operator's safety management system. There are regular and consistent contractor audits undertaken by operators to ensure compliance with the BSEE SEMS mandates and good industry practice. This proposed Coast Guard regulation will create two different safety plans for a single OCS operation by two different regulatory agencies, which makes this proposal not only duplicative, but potentially contradictory and dangerous.

Other Vessel Requirements

These vessels are also required to carry a Vessel General Permit (VGP) regulated by the Environmental Protection Agency (EPA), meet emission standards, abide by procedures for ballast water discharge, update marine safety manuals, conduct life-

34

saving and firefighting drills, undergo annual inspections, and keep up with new versions of these various requirements including equipment mandates and retrofits.

Training Requirements

Our industry is also the subject of increasing and sometime excessive training requirements for crewmembers, which cost boat operators significant amounts of time and money and represent a barrier to recruitment. The Coast Guard published regulations on Christmas Eve last year that amended the Standards of Training, Certification, and Watchkeeping (STCW), requiring additional sea service time for crew members aboard OSVs, medical certificates, and numerous other changes.

Overall Impact of Regulations

The offshore marine industry believes strongly in promoting a culture of safety and environmental responsibility and instills those values into each and every crewmember. For years now the U.S. workboat industry has had a stellar safety record, but OSVs operating in the Gulf of Mexico travel with bookshelves that are continuously loaded down with additional rows of plans, procedures, and manuals required by multiple federal agencies. They are continuing to overlap regulation upon regulation in the offshore environment. This trend not only makes compliance costly and difficult, it threatens to put family-owned boat companies out of business and shift the focus toward paperwork instead of safe operations, which will actually reduce safety instead of improving it.

Workforce Development

Another significant challenge we are facing on the marine service side is workforce development. Although the Gulf region has a very skilled industrial workforce, it's an aging one, and we are struggling to feed the pipeline. The average age of a welder in U.S. shipyards is 55. Given the aging mariner and shipyard workforce, increased funding and utilization of Department of Labor grants for training, advancement, and retention is needed, such as the State of Louisiana's Incumbent Worker program. Vessel operators are having a tough time recruiting new talent, and it's a shame because these are good paying, steady jobs that give students straight out of high school a chance to earn upward of 50, 60, or even 100 thousand dollars within 4 or 5 years.

Partnering with technical and community colleges is important, but we need to do more. We need to get into the elementary schools and the high schools and explain the incredible economic potential of these industrial jobs. Not all of our high schools should be college preparatory schools. We need to introduce trade skills into the curriculum on a wider basis and give kids the option to attend full-time trade schools if they choose. Coastal Louisiana parishes enjoy some of the lowest unemployment rates in the country, but the maritime industry is still struggling to fill positions. High-paying jobs aren't being filled because not enough children are exposed to industry opportunities in the local economy or given a chance to attain skills to succeed in that industry. We need deckhands and welders, but we need engineers too, and science, technology, engineering, and math (STEM) programs at all age levels in this region of the country should also expose students more regularly to the offshore energy and marine industries that anchor South Louisiana's economy.

Conclusion

In closing, I'll give you some information about my company that I am especially proud of. We have a loyal and dedicated workforce of some of the greatest Americans alive. Over 300 employees work for Aries Marine and they enjoy salaries that can support a family along with rich benefits of medical insurance, supplemental insurance, and a 401K retirement savings account. A great package in any industry but the phenomenal thing is we provide the families medical benefits, too. Through Aries Marine over 900 people enjoy the comforts of medical insurance. That's what this industry does for America.

Thank you again for the opportunity to share my perspective on some of the opportunities and challenges faced by the offshore marine industry. I'd be happy to answer any questions.

The CHAIR. Thank you, Mr. Ramsay. Excellent.
Mr. Malbrough.

STATEMENT OF ONEIL MALBROUGH, CB&I, DIRECTOR OF COASTAL, PORTS AND MARINE, ENVIRONMENT AND INFRA-STRUCTURE

Mr. MALBROUGH. First I'd like to thank you, Madame Chair, for allowing me to speak at this hearing and to talk about a critical issue that our local, coastal energy ports have been wrestling with for more than a decade. My name is Oneil Malbrough. I'm the Director of the Coastal, Ports and Marine Group for CB and I.

The Coastal Ports and Marine Group is the engineering and construction management group for CBI that specializes in engineering and design of ports, channels, port infrastructure and marine towns.

The presentation I will make today is centered on the opportunities and challenges that are currently occurring to a group of ports in Louisiana we call the Coastal Energy Ports.

These ports are very unique in that they do not ship containers, corn, steel or ore, but what they do ship is personnel, supplies, platforms, equipment and numerous other sophisticated and complex machinery components to and from the offshore drilling rigs and production platforms in the Gulf. To be more precise, these energy ports facilitate the day to day operations of a multibillion dollar industry by delivering the necessary supplies and equipment needed to explore, drill and produce a large percentage of our oil and gas consumed by our Nation.

Just to detail the magnitude of the type of infrastructure I'm talking about these floating and fixed structures are comparable to thousands of small cities scattered across the thousands of square miles of the Gulf of Mexico which require daily support from these land base facilities.

The oil and gas industry in the Gulf of Mexico started in the 1940s in the shallow waters along our coast. In the following few decades the industry continued to move farther and farther out on the shelf. As you are well aware has expanded into waters over 10,000 feet deep and 100 plus miles offshore.

As the drilling rigs and production platforms move farther and farther, the size and weight of the equipment required to explore, drill, fabricate and install and produce for our Nation so critically depends on, keeps getting bigger and bigger.

The first slide I will share with you today depicts the different types of production facilities that the industry has used in the Gulf over the past 60 years. As you can see everything is getting bigger and bigger. Unfortunately as this oil and gas infrastructure has grown in size and weight, our ports, more specifically the coastal energy ports, have not been able to keep up primarily due to the insufficient water depths that navigate to and from as well as within the ports.

I would like to emphasize that in the 1950s, 1960s and 1970s, almost every piece of iron floating and working in the Gulf of Mexico was built and serviced by the ports along the Gulf Coast. However today, industry experts will tell you that the number is closer to 60 to 70 percent and getting worse. The 30 to 40 percent drop off is directly related to the slow and continuous restrictions in our access channels to the Gulf which are the main arteries that supply the lifeblood to the heart of our local economy and our Nation's energy supplies.

Being capable or incapable of servicing the deep water growth in the Gulf will be the No. 1, most vital component to the economic future of our Nation's energy ports. Without deeper channels we cannot and will not survive.

Slide 2.

The next slide depicts the 22 coastal ports connected to the Gulf in Louisiana. These ports are divided into 3 geographical regions with the Western and Eastern regions centered around the Calcasieu and Mississippi River respectively.

The next slide which is the Central region gives us an in depth look at what we refer to as the Coastal Energy Port corridor. It extends from Freshwater Bayou in the southwest portion of the State to the Barataria Waterway in the southeast portion of the State.

This corridor includes the Ports of Vermillion.

The Port of Delcambre.

The Port of Iberia.

The Port of West St. Mary.

The Port of Morgan City.

The Port of Terrebonne.

I'm going to mess it up. Is it the Port of Iberia?

The Port of Morgan City.

The Port of Terrebonne.

The Port of Grand Isle.

The Port of Fouchon.

Although the previous slides show the robust industrial activity currently going on within our coastal energy ports it is very hard to illustrate the magnitude of what these 9 coastal energy ports mean to our national economy and the growth potential if they had the proper channel depth to fully service the channels of the current industry operating in the Gulf and even more so for the industry on the horizon that will be operating in the Gulf in the future.

If there's a baby boomer message I'd like to get across today in this discussion it would be that our grandfather's channels are not deep enough for our children's offshore oil and gas industry.

Whereby a 12 foot draft was adequate for the GIWW Freshwater Bayou Commercial Canal and Barataria Waterway when they were dug in the 1950s and 15 and 20 and 25 foot draft were OK for Terrebonne and Morgan City and Fouchon, respectively, when they were dug in the 1960s. They are not adequate for the industry of today. If nothing is done it will cause detrimental effects on the growth of the industry of the future.

All of the mainline from Freshwater Bayou to Barataria Waterway need to be a minimum of 20 feet deep and Fouchon needs to be somewhere between 35 and 50 foot deep to adequately handle the industry today and the industry of the future.

Studies have shown that the Coastal Energy Port corridor is home to nearly 40,000 direct jobs and 36,000 indirect jobs in and around the area where they are located. Economists have estimated that a billion and a half dollars in construction projects have been lost in the last few years due to insufficient water depth. Estimates show that with sufficient water depth we could see 35 to 40 percent increase in direct jobs and 14,000 indirect jobs throughout ports in surrounding areas.

With these increases direct benefits within—with these increases direct benefits not only to the respective regions, the investment in deeper channels would also benefit the Nation as a whole by reducing our dependence on foreign oil, reducing our trade deficit, reducing the flow of money to some unstable and unfriendly areas of the world and providing a more reliable and cheaper energy supply at home that could reverse the decline in domestic manufacturing jobs that have occurred for more than a generation.

In the current projection for deep water exploration in the Gulf are accurate this State and this Nation needs to get together and figure out a way to get these channels dredged and maintained and to do so in haste. If we don't then we'll once again miss the opportunity of a lifetime.

It can't go without saying that there has been some positive steps that have been taken by Congress and the Federal delegation in our State in the past few years toward the deepening of the channel for the Ports of Iberia, Terrebonne and Fouchon. But there is much left to be done in getting these channels dredged deeper and properly maintained and to interconnect all the other 6 coastal ports into the system. I'm hoping that the attention given to this critical infrastructure issue by this committee today is another step forward in moving our coastal energy ports closer to the size and depth required for the industry they support.

Once again I would like to thank you for allowing me to speak today on behalf of these coastal energy ports.

[The prepared statement of Mr. Malbrough follows:]

PREPARED STATEMENT OF MR. ONEIL MALBROUGH, CB&I, DIRECTGOR OF COASTAL, PORTS AND MARINE

1First, I'd like to thank Senator Landrieu and the Committee for allowing me to speak at this hearing and to talk about a critical issue that our local Coastal Energy Ports have been wrestling with for more than a decade. My name is Oneil Malbrough and I am the Director of the Coastal, Ports and Marine Group for CB&I. The Coastal, Ports and Marine Group is the Engineering and Construction Management Group within CB&I that specializes in the Planning, Engineering and Design of Ports, Channels, Port Infrastructure and Marine Terminals in many different parts of the world.

The presentation I will make today is centered on the Opportunities and Challenges that are currently occurring to a group of Ports in Louisiana, we call the "Coastal Energy Ports". These Ports are very unique in that they do not ship containers, or corn, or steel, or ore; but what they do ship is personnel, supplies, platforms, equipment and numerous other sophisticated and complex machinery components to and from offshore drilling rigs and production platforms in the Gulf of Mexico. To be more precise, these Energy Ports facilitate the day to day operations of a multi-billion dollar industry by delivering the necessary supplies and equipment needed to explore, drill, and produce a large percentage of the oil and gas consumed by our nation. Just to detail the magnitude of the type of infrastructure I am talking about, these floating and fixed structures are comparable to thousands of small cities scattered across thousands of square miles of the Gulf of Mexico which require daily support from these land based facilities.

The offshore oil and gas industry in the Gulf of Mexico started in the 1940's, in the shallow waters along our coast, and in the following few decades, the industry continued to move farther and farther out on the shelf and now, as you are well aware, has expanded into waters over 10,000 feet deep and 100+ miles offshore. As the drilling rigs and production platforms move farther into the deeper waters of the Gulf of Mexico, the size and weight of the equipment required to explore, drill, fabricate, install and produce the oil and gas that our nation so critically depends on, keeps getting bigger and bigger.

(Slide 1) The first slide I will share with you today depicts the different types of production facilities that the industry has used in the Gulf of Mexico over the pass 60+years. As you can see everything is getting bigger and bigger. Unfortunately, as this oil and gas infrastructure has grown in size and weight, our Ports, more specifically the Coastal Energy Ports, have not been able to keep up, primarily due to the insufficient water depths that navigate to and from, as well as within our Ports.

I would like to emphasize that in the 1950's, 60's and 70's almost every piece of iron floating and working in the Gulf of Mexico was built and serviced by the Ports along the Gulf Coast. However today, industry experts will tell you that the number is closer to 60—70 percent and getting worse. This 30 percent to 40 percent drop off is directly related to the slow and continuous restrictions on our access channels to the Gulf of Mexico, which are the main arteries that supply the "life blood" to the heart of our local economy and our nation's energy supplies. Being capable or incapable of servicing the Deepwater Growth in the Gulf of Mexico will be the number one most vital component to the economic future of our nation's energy ports. Without deeper channels we cannot and will not survive!

(Slide 2) The next slide depicts all the Coastal Ports in Louisiana (22) connected to the Gulf of Mexico. These Ports are divided into three (3) geographical regions, with the Western & Eastern Regions centered around the Calcasieu River and Mississippi River, respectively.

(Slide 3) This next slide, which is in the Central Region, gives an in depth look at what we refer to as our Coastal Energy Port corridor. It extends from Freshwater Bayou, in the southwest portion of the State, to the Barataria Bay Waterway, in the southeast portion of the State. This corridor includes the following Ports:

> (1) Port of Vermillion (including Intracoastal City) (Slide 4, 5, and 6)
> (2) Port of Delcambre
> (3) Port of Iberia (Slide 7 and 8)
> (4) Port of West St. Mary
> (5) Port of Morgan City (Slide 9)
> (6) Port of Terrebonne (Slide 10 and 11)
> (7) Lockport/Larose Marine Industrial Complex
> (8) Port of Grand Isle (Slide 12)
> (9) Port Fouchon (Slide 13, 14, and 15)

Although the previous slides show the robust industrial activity currently going on in our Coastal Energy Ports, it's very hard to illustrate the magnitude of what these 9 Coastal Energy Ports mean to our national economy and the growth potential if they had the proper channel depths to fully service the demands of the current industry operating in the Gulf today and even more so for the industry on the horizon that will be operating in the Gulf in the very near future.

If there's a "baby boomer" message that I'd like to get across today in this discussion, it would be that "Our Grandfather's channels are not deep enough for our Children's offshore oil and gas industry". Whereby a 12' draft was adequate for the GIWW, Freshwater Bayou, Commercial Canal and Barataria Bay Waterway when they were dug in the 50's and 15', 20' and 25' draft were OK for Terrebonne, Morgan City and Fouchon respectively when they were dug in the 60's, they are not adequate for the industry of today and if nothing is done, it will cause detrimental effects on the growth of the industry of the future. All of the mainline channels from Freshwater Bayou to Barataria Bay Waterway need to be at a minimum of 20' deep and Port Fouchon needs to be 35'-50' deep to adequately handle the industry today and the industry of the future.

Studies have shown that the Coastal Energy Port Corridor is home to nearly 40,000 direct jobs and impacts an additional 36,000 indirect jobs in and around the areas where they are located. Economists have estimated that > $1.5B in construction projects have been lost in the last few years due to insufficient water depths. Estimates show that with sufficient water depths, we could see a 35—40 percent increase in direct jobs (15,000 jobs) and 14,000 additional indirect jobs at our ports and the surrounding areas.

While these increases will directly benefit their respective regions, the investment in deeper channels will also benefit the nation as a whole by:

- Reducing our dependence on foreign oil,
- Reducing our trade deficit,
- Reducing the flow of money to some unstable and unfriendly areas of the world, and
- Providing a more reliable and cheaper energy supply at home that could reverse the decline in domestic manufacturing jobs that has occurred for more than a generation.

If the current projections for Deepwater Exploration in the Gulf of Mexico are accurate, this State and this Nation needs to get together and figure out a way to get these channels dredged and maintained and to do so in haste. If we don't then we'll let this "once in a lifetime" opportunity pass us by.

It can't go without saying that there has been some positive steps that have been taken by the Congress, our Federal Delegation and our State in the past few years toward the deepening of the channels for the Ports of Iberia, Terrebonne and Fouchon, but there is much left to be done in getting these channels dredged deeper and properly maintained and to interconnect all the other 6 coastal ports into the system. I am hoping that the attention given to this critical infrastructure issue by this committee today is another step forward in moving our Coastal Energy Ports closer to the size and depth required by the industry they support.

(Slide 16) Once again, I would like to thank you for allowing me to speak to you today on behalf of our Coastal Energy Ports.

The CHAIR. Thank you. Excellent testimony.

Mr. Chiasson.

Go ahead and take a minute to set up.

Oh, well, we'll try to get it unstuck. But why don't you go ahead. Do you want to do it by slides or we'll follow here?

STATEMENT OF CHETT CHIASSON, EXECUTIVE DIRECTOR, GREATER LAFOUCHE PORT COMMISSION, GALLIANO, LA

Mr. CHIASSON. There's some right there.

The CHAIR. Go ahead. You can begin and if there's—Bubba will find them for me.

Mr. CHIASSON. At the end of it there's some slides. Oh, there you go. That's it right there.

The CHAIR. OK, got it.

Mr. CHIASSON. We have it.

The CHAIR. OK.

Mr. CHIASSON. OK.

Good afternoon, Chairwoman Landrieu. I very much appreciate the invitation to appear before you today and as always for your continued leadership.

Senator, I know you know Port Fourchon. That it services 90 percent of all the deep water activity in the U.S. Gulf of Mexico, Louisiana offshore oil port and nearly 20 percent of the Nation's oil supply. I know that if I'm appearing before you anywhere at any time I better mention the critical need to complete the remaining portions of Louisiana Highway 1, the only landside link to Port Fourchon and the rest of the world and the critical need for the Federal Government, in this case the Corps of Engineers, to maintain and deepen, where needed, the channels and our Nation's ports.

Port Fourchon and LA 1 are prime examples of the need to maintain our Nation's infrastructure to support a variety of economic activities in our country.

But today I'd like to focus my comments on the role that the Federal Government plays in offshore energy development of all kinds through its leasing program, development of its 5 year plan and the like. At the end of the day nothing else matters without the Federal Government promoting and effectively managing offshore energy development. All of the economic activities that fuels our local and national economies, all of the jobs, all of the energy independence we seek to achieve, all of the benefits that we see now and hope to continue well past any of our lifetimes, start when an effective, consistent, reliable offshore leasing program.

I'd like to direct your attention to the 3 photographs that I brought with me today.

The first one is an aerial photograph on the left side of the slide of Port Fourchon in the early 1990s, in 1993 before the Deep Water Royalty Relief Act was passed in 1995.

The second photograph is of the port today. This was taken just this past January. It's already a little out of date. We are growing just that fast.

The third, if we can move it to the next?

Oh, OK, sorry.

Oh, OK.

The third is just a map depicting what we're looking at into the future. You can see an extra slip out there and moving forward into the future to develop more to service the oil and gas industry.

With this newest expansion we will grow the port by an additional 300 lease able acres over our current 12 hundred leased acre footprint today. These 3 photographs, spanning roughly 30 years, illustrate the growth of Port Fourchon as a direct result of energy exploration and development in the Gulf. Our growth, of course, is directly linked to the investment by a multitude of companies involved in offshore energy, exploration and development which, of course, is impacted by the Federal Government both positively and negatively.

You don't need to look back any further than 1995 when Congress passed the Royalty Relief Act to see the positive effect of Federal policy in fostering the growth in offshore energy development that we experience today.

On the flip side of that, we have the tragedy of the Deep Water Horizon incident, the likes of which I pray we will never see again which resulted, as you well know, in the offshore moratorium and establishment of a new permitting regime which while necessary and I presumed well intended, took a long time to develop and implement both of which caused additional economic hardship and delay in further investment, seriously impacting the economic growth that comes with it.

Now our industry is as resilient as it is innovative. Thus we have not only rebounded since Mercando, but we are looking toward the future once again. By looking, I mean investing tens of billions of dollars across this industry.

As speaking of one of those investors on behalf of my port, investing public funds, our industry needs to have confidence that the investments made in domestic offshore energy production will not be overly impeded by Federal actions or inactions, as the case may be, and that our Nation's domestic energy policy, now and over the next century, will continue to sustain industry investment of all types today, tomorrow and years to come.

Senator, I'd like to provide you with one recent example that's really not on the headlines right now, but I assure you will have the very kind of positive benefits that our industry looks for with respect to the Federal Government's role in offshore energy development.

I'm talking about the U.S. and Mexico Transboundary Agreement. This agreement is intended to facilitate the development of oil and gas reservoirs that cross the International Maritime Boundary between our two countries in the Gulf of Mexico. That means that additional work is coming for U.S. companies in the oil field service and supply industry and for Port Fourchon and other oil service ports in the U.S. Gulf. That's great news.

Along those lines we now know that BOEM currently is requesting comments on the development of the 5-year plan to take effect in 2017. As someone who sees, literally on a daily basis, the positive results of Federal lease sales, as someone who is currently planning in investing in Gulf activity over the coming decades, I can state that a 5-year plan must present a robust OCS leasing program, promote expanded access in areas of the Gulf and in Alaska currently available for leasing and promote new areas for lease off our coastlines as well.

I can tell you as a Port Director for the most important offshore service port in our country I have had a number of conversations with port directors or other community leaders around the country interested in how and what makes Port Fourchon tick and so have the vessel companies and other service companies that work at Port Fourchon and elsewhere in the Gulf. Communities as well as small and large businesses are preparing to invest in new areas where offshore energy activity will be permitted. I don't just mean oil and gas activities, renewable energy as well. We have one local company at Lafourche Parish called Michael Offshore that is actually certified to do this work and has done some on the Atlantic Coast.

For Port Fourchon to continue to grow and have a successful future creating jobs continued Gulf of Mexico lease sales are critically important. That is the future of our industry. Robust lease sales have the ability to energize oil and gas service companies that suppliers and so on throughout the country.

Port Fourchon should be seen as an example of what could happen in areas along the east and west coast and what must continue in our own backyard if these areas would be available for conventional and renewable energy development.

Thank you.

[The prepared statement of Mr. Chiasson follows:]

PREPARED STATEMENT OF CHETT CHIASSON, EXECUTIVE DIRECTOR, GREATER LAFOUCHE PORT COMMISSION, GALLIANO, LA

Good afternoon Chairwoman Landrieu and Members of the Committee. I appreciate the opportunity to appear before you today. My name is Chett Chiasson, and I am the Executive Director of the Greater Lafourche Port Commission, otherwise known as Port Fourchon.

With this testimony, I hope to impress upon Members of the Committee and the federal officials appearing here today several points: the importance of Port Fourchon to the offshore oil and gas industry; the contribution that Port Fourchon therefore makes to the national economy; and the importance of robust oil and gas lease sales in the Gulf of Mexico, to not just the Gulf economy and not just with respect to offshore fossil fuel development, but to our national economy, and to sustain long term, offshore energy development from all available sources that our Country intends to pursue.

By way of background, The Greater Lafourche Port Commission, a political subdivision of the state of Louisiana, facilitates the economic growth of the communities in which it operates by maximizing the flow of trade and commerce. We do this to grow our economy and preserve our environment and heritage. The Port Commission exercises jurisdiction over the Tenth Ward of Lafourche Parish, south of the Intracoastal Waterway, including Port Fourchon and the South Lafourche Leonard Miller, Jr. Airport. The Port Commission has been in existence since 1960 and its 9 member Board of Commissioners is the only elected Port Commission in the State of Louisiana.

Port Fourchon is located on the Gulf of Mexico, near the mouth of Bayou Lafourche, and it is the only Louisiana port directly on the Gulf of Mexico. Although more than 500 million barrels of domestically produced and imported crude oil per year are transported via pipelines through the Port, Port Fourchon does not handle any bulk oil and gas per se. Rather, we are an intermodal offshore supply port. More than 250 companies utilize Port Fourchon in servicing offshore rigs in the Gulf of Mexico, carrying equipment, supplies and personnel to offshore locations. In terms of service, Port Fourchon's tenants provide services to 90 percent of all deepwater rigs in the Gulf of Mexico, and roughly 45 percent of all shallow water rigs in the Gulf. 80 percent of all Gulf oil now comes from deepwater Gulf of Mexico operations. In total, Port Fourchon plays a key role in nearly 20 percent of the nation's entire oil supply.

A study of the economic impact of Port Fourchon to the Nation determined that more than $63 billion in total value of oil and gas are associated with Port Fourchon. A more recent study published by the U.S. Department of Homeland Security's NISAC Lab in collaboration with the NIMSAT Institute, entitled the Louisiana Highway 1/Port Fourchon Study, found that a disruption of access to Port Fourchon for a 90 day period could have a nearly $8 billion impact to the Nation's GDP. While each report was intended for different purposes, I share this information with the Committee to illustrate the need for continued and sustained progress in developing all of our offshore energy resources, both conventional and non-conventional. Port Fourchon is the epicenter of offshore oil and gas activities, and the companies in and around Fourchon, and their technologies and innovations developed as a result of these activities, will not only continue to sustain future offshore domestic oil and gas activities, but will foster growth in our budding offshore renewable energy industry as well.

For Port Fourchon to continue to grow and have a successful future creating jobs throughout the economy and facilitating development for our community, continued Gulf of Mexico Lease sales are critically important. That is the future of the oil and gas industry. Robust lease sales have the ability to energize oil and gas service companies', their suppliers and their suppliers' suppliers throughout the country, who are planning for future development. It facilitates critically needed investment by entities that service these offshore activities, which has a positive ripple effect throughout the national economy.

According to the economic impact study to which I eluded earlier, Port Fourchon supports more than 8,000 direct jobs. These are good paying jobs, in which someone with a high school diploma can start out making $50,000 per year. If that person wants to work on an offshore supply vessel or tugboat company, they can start out as a deckhand and work their way up to Captain within 5 years, earning a six figure income. The Houma-Thibodaux MSA maintains one of the lowest unemployment rates in the country, at about 3.7 percent, well below the National average. If a man or woman is willing and able to work, they typically have a job. And I know this is the case in other Gulf communities, and in areas around the country where new discoveries of onshore energy resources have occurred, such as in North Dakota, or eastern states such as Pennsylvania, West Virginia and Ohio.

A very recent example of the role that the federal government can play in fostering continued economic development in the US, coupled with achieving further energy independence, is the U.S. Mexico Transboundary Agreement. This agreement is intended to facilitate the development of oil and gas reservoirs that cross the international maritime boundary between the U.S. and Mexico in the Gulf. The Department of Interior signed an agreement with Mexico in 2012, and implementing legislation was enacted by Congress at the end of last year and signed into law by President Obama. Just about a month ago, at the end of May, BOEM awarded the first leases—three to be exact, in an area of the Gulf subject to the Transboundary Agreement. Without this Agreement, the ability to develop this area—and more importantly, what US laws would apply and what US companies would be able to participate in this new activity, were uncertain at best. Thus the ratification of this agreement will have significant economic benefits to US companies who participate in the oil and gas industry. And I assure this Committee, as I know for a fact, additional work is coming for Port Fourchon and other oil service ports in the U.S. Gulf as a result. This is good news and congratulations to all in our federal government who achieved this goal.

43

The Bureau of Ocean Energy Management (BOEM) is currently requesting comments on the development of the next five year plan for offshore energy development, to take effect in 2017. As someone who sees, literally on a daily basis, the results of federal lease sales, and as someone who is currently planning and investing in Gulf activity over the coming decades, I can state that a five year plan must present a robust OCS leasing program, promote expanded access in not only areas of the Gulf and in Alaska, but expanded areas off our coastlines as well. I can tell you that as the Port Director for the most important offshore service port in our Country, I have had a number of conversations with port directors or other community leaders around the country, interested in how and what makes Port Fourchon tick. So have the vessel companies and other service companies that work at Fourchon and elsewhere in the Gulf. These aren't just academic conversations. Communities and small and large businesses are preparing to invest in areas where offshore energy activity is permitted. And I don't mean just oil and gas. One of the leading service companies working today on offshore wind development on the East Coast is a liftboat company in Lafourche Parish that was started in the 1960's to work the offshore oil fields, and to this day continues to work on offshore oil and gas projects in the Gulf. But it now owns three new liftboats that are certified to work on offshore wind projects as well as oil and gas. Thus it only makes sense that those companies involved in offshore mineral development will play similar roles in offshore renewable energy development, as we're seeing that already.

In conclusion, while the effects of the BP oil spill, the subsequent moratorium and the new permitting regime still linger, our industry is as resilient as it is innovative, and thus we have not only rebounded, but are looking towards the future. And by "looking", I mean investing tens of billions of dollars across this industry. But the industry needs to have confidence that the investments made in domestic offshore energy production will not be overly impeded by governmental regulations, and that our Nation's domestic energy policy will continue to sustain investment of all energy types. The response by industry in recent government lease sales is certainly one indicator of that confidence, and the significant sums of dollars then invested as part of those sales.

Port Fourchon should be seen as an example of what could happen in areas along the East and West Coasts if these areas would be available for conventional and renewable energy development, as well as continue to explore in areas of the Gulf and Alaska already open for development. Billions of dollars of investment throughout the country, low unemployment rates, high paying jobs, more revenue for our federal and local governments, and making great strides toward energy independence.

Again Senator Landrieu and Members of the Committee, I appreciate the opportunity to appear before you today, and I would be happy to answer any questions that the Committee may have.

The CHAIR. Thank you all very much for that excellent testimony.

Let me begin, if I could, Mr. Satterlee, with you.

In your testimony you said that of the off limit OCS areas Shell may be particularly interested or focused on the Eastern Gulf of Mexico and the Mid Southern Atlantic areas. Can you express why Shell might be interested in those areas and what potential do you all see in the Eastern Gulf and Mid South Atlantic areas?

Mr. SATTERLEE. Yes.

Let me just preface it by saying that we are in a quiet period so I'm limited on forward looking information.

The CHAIR. Correct.

Mr. SATTERLEE. Some of the information is proprietary. But— and you asked a question earlier of the government representatives concerning seismic data. There is quite a bit of seismic data in the Atlantic and also in the Eastern Gulf of Mexico.

In the Atlantic though it's more than 3 decades old and it does not go very far deep, in deep water. So it only goes out to about maybe, 50 miles out. So we have reprocessed some of that data. What we see is promising.

44

Although we certainly prefer to have new seismic data before we go to a lease sale what we see so far is promising.

The CHAIR. What would be—can you just explain for the record and not in too, too much technical detail, but explain for our audience that may not know the activities that go along with seismic? How would you explain the difference in technology 20 years ago to today? How much more accurate is some of that?

There's some—that's 1.

How much more accurate, generally, is it by industry standards?

Are there any—there are some legitimate criticisms of some impacts that seismic could have on marine life, etcetera. Could you just comment about the state of seismic today in the industry, generally?

Mr. SATTERLEE. I'm not an expert in that area. So I would like to get back to the committee on a more detailed answer.

Mr. SATTERLEE. But there's really two areas where seismic technology has been enhanced over the last several decades.

One, in the acquisition of the seismic. So you've got more precise air guns and more precise receivers.

Then probably even more so is in the interpretation and the work of that data to get it into a format where you can interpret it.

So the limitation for the seismic in the Atlantic is both because it's old, but also because it has not been acquired in deeper water. But also the spacing of the lines is pretty far apart. So we'd like to see much closer spacing of lines so we can make a better interpretation.

With regard to marine mammals the mitigation measures that we have in place today really protect the marine mammals, marine animals. So we understand that there's quite a bit of concern, but there's also quite a bit of science and environmental work going on right now to make sure that we do not harm those animals.

The CHAIR. OK.

You testified also about some of the performance based regulatory oversight programs that Shell believes would be most effective. Can you give an example or 2 of the kind of performance based regulatory programs that would be?

You all drill all over the world.

Mr. SATTERLEE. Correct.

The CHAIR. So you might answer this by giving us, giving the committee, 1 or 2 examples of what other Nations do that have high environmental standards or at least standards equivalent to ours and maybe a more efficient system that we could look to as a model.

Mr. SATTERLEE. OK.

The crux of the matter is that the regulatory process works very slowly here in the United States. It's a good system, but it takes anywhere from 3 to 7 years to get a new set of regulations in place. Our move into deep water and the technology development has moved much quicker than that.

So basically, the regulatory agencies just have not been able to keep pace. That's no fault of our own. It's really the process that we have.

So what a performance based system enables an agency to do is to move much faster than their own regulatory development process. It can be managed through industry standards. So industry standards can be done. Then our industry will be subject to those standards because they can be incorporated and made requirements.

As far as other Nations I think Norway and Australia have both excellent systems. To their credit BSEE and BOEM are very much involved in an International Regulators Forum which compares data and also it compares regulatory systems. So I know they're looking at types of regulatory reforms.

But I will say that the SEMS program that BSEE has in place right now is a very good example of a performance based system.

The CHAIR. Great.

Mr. Leimkuhler, could you add to that as a—you know, here you have a large, international, public company. You all are the largest private, you know, operator. What perspective would you like to share on this potentially improved regulatory framework?

Mr. LEIMKUHLER. I would second what Ken said, a more of a performance standard where in the regulations you describe the risks that we are challenged to meet and then we come up with a set of operating protocol procedures, SEMS plans, to actually meet that risk rather than a more prescriptive approach.

I think a good example of that would be on blow out preventer testing.

Right now we're required to do almost a full overhaul of the BOPs every time they come to surface. So at LLOG we're in a development program. I've got sequential completions lined up where I'm going to do the completions for that facility I showed you on the slide.

I've got 5 wells ready to complete. Each completion takes about 30 days. But every time I bring my BOP stack to the surface I have to fully break it down. That's 14 days worth of work when I'm only using it for 30.

There is a sweet spot about 100 to 150 days where your BOP is extremely reliable. You can make an argument it's actually from a risk based perspective better to leave it down and hop the BOP from well to well. BSEE is starting to be amenable to looking at those types of proposals, but in response to the current regulations of the new rig I have coming into the Gulf, we have spent an additional $30 million to put a second BOP on so that we can efficiently operate and do those 5 wells back to back to where I'll be cycling those BOPs from the surface to the sea floor.

So that's a pretty direct impact.

The CHAIR. That's a very good example of a regulation that might be an over reach and not necessary. It may, eventually, do more harm than good. We've got to let the engineers figure that out.

Mr. LEIMKUHLER. Correct.

The CHAIR. Let me ask you, Mr. Malbrough, really try to help us get on to this record the gap between the dredging, not just the dredging depths from 12 to 20 or 15 to 25, but the financial gap that we're looking at.

I don't know if you have the data. You talked about the 9 ports that you might have data for. But there are, of course, upwards,

I think, of maybe 20 energy ports in the coast from Alabama to Texas.

But let's just focus either on the 9 that you're most familiar with or some subset of those that you're comfortable with to give this committee some information about how short we are on our dredging dollars. So you could take it from Port Fourchon.

What is your dredging requirement annually?

What do you receive from the Federal and State government?

What is the delta?

But I'm looking for a total amount from the 9 energy ports that you had in your testimony, roughly?

Mr. MALBROUGH. When we added up the annual requirements that the corps had projected, if I'm not mistaken, with the exception of Morgan City the $10 million to $12 million that is allocated now is probably adequate.

Morgan City because it's inside the Atchafalaya River and it has a significant amount of sediment moving down there by itself is $15 million.

So we have always talked about somewhere between $25 and $30 million a year would sufficiently dredge the channels to their existing depths.

The CHAIR. To those 9 ports.

Mr. MALBROUGH. To maintain.

The CHAIR. To maintain those 9.

Mr. MALBROUGH. Those 9.

The CHAIR. Ports.

How much do you receive from either the State or the Federal Government?

Mr. MALBROUGH. It's usually around $10 to $12 million depending upon—last year you all had that supplemental, I don't know what you call it, the supplemental.

The CHAIR. So you're basically getting half of what you need?

Mr. MALBROUGH. That's correct.

The CHAIR. Roughly, for those ports.

Mr. MALBROUGH. We're not yet—that's correct.

When you—the idea is there some people—when people miss a year and then they catch them up a year or 2 later. So it's a matter of having about half as much money to do the job that they need. The idea is that we would need double that at this time to keep them to their authorized depths today.

The CHAIR. Which one of you testified that the lack of this relatively small amount of money. I mean as the Federal Government's budget goes, $25 to $30 million is significant for us, but not significant.

The loss of jobs, one of you testified how many jobs have we lost or what contracts have we lost. Was that you, Neil?

Mr. MALBROUGH. Yes.

The CHAIR. Can you repeat that, please?

Mr. MALBROUGH. But that was not because of the dredging cycle that was because of the lack of being able—those local contractors are not able to even bid on projects because of their inadequate draft depth to show the delivery of some of the big platforms.

The CHAIR. You said we lost, according to your testimony, about a billion and a half dollars?

Mr. MALBROUGH. That's correct. Actually it was three and a half years now.

But in the meantime the unauthorized—the lack of O and M dredging is in every single channel in that 9 coastal ports, except for the one. The 6-months after the Corps finishes dredging all of those channels are inadequate. OK?

There is not one of those channels with the exception of Port Fourchon, OK. Port Fourchon is the deepest. But it's closer to the Gulf and has a minimum amount.

The CHAIR. Oh, I see. So let's be clear.

So you're saying even with the—we're short $10 to $12 billion—million a year to keep these channels dredged to their authorized, but their authorized is still not sufficient to attract the 1.5——

Mr. MALBROUGH. Five billion dollar reconstruction price.

The CHAIR. Five billion dollars.

So what we want to get into this committee for the staff is the delta of the dredging to the authorized level annually for all energy ports in the Gulf.

Then what the cost would be to get them all up to your children's deep water, not your grandfather's deep water energy industry.

Mr. MALBROUGH. That's correct.

The CHAIR. That's what we need for this.

Chett, do you want to—I mean, Mr. Chiasson, do you want to add anything?

Mr. CHIASSON. You can call me Chett, Senator.

The CHAIR. OK.

[Laughter.]

Mr. CHIASSON. I'd just like to say that, just kind of echoing what Oneil was talking about when it comes to dredging of Port Fourchon. We're very happy to say that the Corps does its job for us. Fortunately enough for Port Fourchon we don't really have a siltation issue unless we have a storm that comes by. But we don't have sediment coming down by Lafourche to deposit into our channel.

So we're fortunate on that fact. But we have, probably, every 3 years a million and a half or so dollars—what was that, to $3 million that's spent in our channel. When we talk about Port Fourchon, we're talking about deepening to continue to meet the demand for the industry.

We already service about 90 percent of all the deep water activity in the Gulf, like I mentioned. In order for us to continue to do so we need to do whatever it is we possibly can to get, you know, at least to 35 feet if not more to be able to handle the size vessels and for the companies, the vessel companies like Mr. Ramsay here, to be able to build those vessels to the capabilities that they really need in the U.S. waters.

The CHAIR. Mr. Ramsay, let me turn it over to you because I think this, this frame, is so important for this committee to really understand and trying to get this onto the Congressional record.

The offshore industry, which is serviced by Port Fourchon primarily in the Gulf, but there are a few other ports that contribute, Corpus Christi in Texas and a few others have needs, have infrastructure needs. $20 million, $30 million annually together. We're going to try to get that figure because it's important to get the official figure.

The reason I press this is because the industry itself generates the tax dollars for the Federal Government. I believe of somewhere between $8 and $10 billion a year. I want the staff to give me the last 3 years right now. You can Google it. The last 3 years of offshore production that's gone to the Federal Government. We're going to get that on this record right now.

But it's somewhere between $8 and $10 billion. So my question to you, Mr. Ramsay, is do you think the Federal Government can afford to spend a few million dollars supporting the ports that generate the $10 billion a year for the——

Is there any reason, as a business person, that you could even see or surmise that the Federal Government would not want to make that decision?

Mr. RAMSAY. Madame Chair, it's not understood at all by Americans why the Federal Government would not want to invest this money into our industry. It makes no sense to us at all.

The CHAIR. Because again, the industry generates, we think, we're going to get the exact numbers in just a minute. But tell me about, again, about what your industry not only employs, but other companies like yours?

Mr. RAMSAY. You know, as I said earlier, we've got currently 4 vessels under construction here and in Louisiana alone that's, you know, about a $90 million investment alone just in construction costs of vessels, the shipyards that we're using collectively employ 700 people, conservatively. You know, those are good paying jobs, you know, great skilled labor jobs.

So and our vendors stretch all across the entire United States. We're buying equipment from, you know, folks in many different States.

Our crews largely come from the Gulf Coast, but many of our officers fly in for crew changes. We've got, you know, engineers and captains that come from as far away as California or Maine to catch a crew change for our vessels. So——

The CHAIR. They take those paychecks back to where?

Mr. RAMSAY. Back to their home States.

The CHAIR. To Maine and to California.

Mr. RAMSAY. Exactly.

Mr. Leimkuhler, as the largest, as one of the largest, independent can you talk about why the Federal Government would not want to make this investment of money that's generated by the industry so that the industry could continue generating the income for the Federal Government based on your subcontractors. You must hire companies like Mr. Ramsay's annual work.

Can you comment about the reach of your contracts? I'm going to ask the same thing of Shell.

Mr. LEIMKUHLER. Yes, our contracts also——

The CHAIR. Speak a little bit, right more directly into the mic.

Mr. LEIMKUHLER. Our contractors span across pretty much the entire country. The Delta House facility we're putting in has contracts existing, I believe it's close to 38 of the 50 States. So it has a national impact. It's a multibillion dollar facility going in place.

Why we can't get the necessary attention to understand the importance of it? I don't know as well.

I think it's a matter of the fact that we, as an industry, to be blunt, probably have done a poor job of selling the Nation on the importance on the role that we actually play. There's a high degree of lack of awareness. I wouldn't' go so far to say ignorance, but maybe that's what—the word that needs to be used.

Just an overall lack of awareness of the role we play, the impact we have and the positive impacts that could be realized if we were able to expand more.

The CHAIR. Mr. Satterlee, for Shell?

Mr. SATTERLEE. We did an after look after we constructed our Perdido platform in the Gulf of Mexico. We found that money that was expended for fabrication was spent by vendors all across the country. I don't have that number in front of me right now, but I can get that for you. Somewhere on the order of a couple billion dollars was spent in other States. So the whole Nation is benefiting from the work that we do here in the Gulf of Mexico.

Mr. SATTERLEE. So to answer your question I think that it's probably just a matter of the rest of the Nation does not understand the benefits that they receive from the work that we do in the Gulf.

The CHAIR. Thank you very much.

Let me see while they're looking for that. I had a couple of other questions.

Let me talk a minute, it's a little off subject, but while I have both of you here about the Jones Act because you testified a little bit on the opposite side of this issue. We have our Offshore Association present.

As you know I'm a strong supporter of the Jones Act. Really believe that we have to do a lot of our boat fabrication business and the law requires that here. But you testified, Mr. Leimkuhler, that in your operations are getting so large that you need some of these heavy lift vessels that are either not built here.

Mr. LEIMKUHLER. Right.

The CHAIR. Are they're not built here? Are they not U.S. manned? Could you explain that?

Mr. Ramsay, I'd like you to comment, although I know this isn't the hearing about the pros and cons of the Jones Act, but I just, since you all are sitting right next to each other I thought I'd get the benefit of your thinking on this.

Mr. LEIMKUHLER. I think—let me recap a recent experience for a discovery we had called power ball where we went to install the facilities.

The top signs that were to be installed on the jack and platform, all of the equipment is hauled to location on U.S. side vessels. But once it arrives it has to be assembled. When we make the lift we can't find U.S. flag vessels capable of making that lift.

So what we had to do in this particular project is we had to actually disassemble the platform into smaller pieces, make more lifts, more complex lifts in order to meet the interpretation of the Jones Act where you have to use a U.S. flag vessel to not only haul the materials to location. That's not been an issue.

But you also must use a U.S. flag vessel to lift and then transport about that 100 feet.

The CHAIR. OK.

Mr. LEIMKUHLER. It's only moving about 100 feet.

The CHAIR. So you're looking for a short—a small exemption.

Mr. LEIMKUHLER. Right.

The CHAIR. To move equipment around, basically, a platform site, not back and forth, but around.

Mr. LEIMKUHLER. Exactly. Once all the vessels are on location just to lift and place. That's all we're asking for.

The CHAIR. Mr. Ramsay.

Mr. RAMSAY. Thank you, Madame Chair, for putting me on the spot. I'm a valued customer.

[Laughter.]

The CHAIR. Good. I'm glad you all aren't the only ones that have difficulty. I do as well with my constituents. So go right ahead.

[Laughter.]

Mr. RAMSAY. Of course as a vessel operator we support a very strong Jones Act. We feel it's a good thing for this Nation, great for our economy, absolutely necessary for our defensive stance around the rest of the world.

You know, I don't have heavy lift vessels. I understand the question that is being discussed here. I think that over the years there has not been a real clear and transparent waiver process to allow the operators to get past this little question.

I think if Homeland Security and Border Patrol, Customs, Border Control and Customs could somehow devise a transparent waiver process to allow that then that would give the customers a chance to make these lifts. It also would indicate to the domestic industry just where we need to go with our construction.

The CHAIR. A limit to—right.

A limit to what could be done or give some signals, a more transparent process.

Mr. RAMSAY. Give us some signals as to what the industry needs as far as equipment and we can build it to make sure that we can do these lifts.

The CHAIR. OK. Thank you all.

Let me give you these numbers.

In 2011 the Federal Government received from offshore alone, $6,442,000,000

In 2013 it was $8.5, $8.6 billion.

In 2014, I think this number went up so it was probably closer to $9 billion. That's annually. So let's just, you know, say, let's rough it at $8 billion, roughly, is what the Federal Government has been receiving each and every year. So over a 10-year period that's $80 billion, when you think about a small percentage of that, 10 percent, 20 percent or 30 percent.

Now the interior States keep 50 percent. OK? That's $40 billion. The interior States would keep and have no restrictions on its expenditure. They have no restrictions.

They can spend it for environmental.

They can spend it not for environmental.

They can spend it for energy or not.

They can spend it for schools, health care.

No restrictions.

But assuming we adopted restrictions to just energy, infrastructure, coastal restoration. What could we do with $40 billion? A lot.

What could we do? Do you want to say what we could do, Mr. Chiasson?

Mr. CHIASSON. We could build LA 1.

The CHAIR. Build LA 1. I could build——

[Laughter.]

Mr. CHIASSON. $300 million, that's it.

The CHAIR. We could build LA 1. We could build I49 South.

Mr. CHIASSON. I49, exactly.

The CHAIR. I49 South. We could do all the dredging we needed to grow and expand the industry in a more safe and, you know, with more safety in mind for workers, for the environment, for businesses. I mean, we could build the flood protection that's necessary. We could restore the marshes.

With 50 percent we could do just an enormous amount. But even with 10 percent of that money or 20 percent of that money, we could do some very important reinvestments back into the region that's producing these riches for the country.

So this has been, I think, an excellent hearing. I'd like to ask each of you all to do just a 30 second wrap up if there's something that you wanted to cover that you didn't.

The record of this hearing will stay open for another 2 weeks which is the custom. We'll receive records from anyone that testified. You want to add addendum to your record or any other individuals that want to add anything to this record.

The CHAIR. I'll be conducting some more field hearings around the country on our next 5 year plan which is 2017 to 2022 OCS plan to make sure we get it right.

What's opened? How it's opened? How the revenues are shared? How those revenues are invested? New regulatory framework that makes the development work more efficiently.

While this hearing was focused on oil and gas development because that's what our region does, there are other types of resource development, wind, some solar opportunities. There's some geothermal opportunities that we're hearing about. I'm going to be asking in other regions of the country, what are some of the other resources that could be developed, energy resources, developed offshore.

If you all have any additional information to share about that, you should submit them in the record.

The CHAIR. But we'll start, maybe, with Mr. Chiasson first and then close with Mr. Satterlee.

Any additional comments, Mr. Chiasson?

Mr. CHIASSON. I just think it's important to point out I wouldn't be a good port director if I didn't point out some of the things when it talks about how important Port Fourchon itself is to our Nation and our national economy.

You talked about other ports along the Gulf Coast and there are significant amount of other ports that service the oil and gas industry, but in a study that you actually helped commission from the Department of Homeland Security back in, I believe, 2011 it came out. It stated that if you combine all the other ports along the Gulf Coast, compare it to Port Fourchon, the services that it can pro-

52

vide. They only match up to 25 percent of the services that Port Fourchon can provide.

So our port——

The CHAIR. To the deep water or to the offshore or deep water?

Mr. CHIASSON. To the offshore oil and gas industry.

The CHAIR. Offshore.

Mr. CHIASSON. So we have 75 percent more capability at Port Fourchon. So we focus solely on the oil and gas industry. So that's the importance there.

You talked about economic impacts and numbers. Our port has about $27 to $30 million in business sales annually. Oh, I'm sorry, daily impact on the national economy. So that's really important to note.

The CHAIR. Excellent.

Mr. CHIASSON. Thank you.

The CHAIR. Neil?

Mr. MALBROUGH. One of the things I'd like to add is just when in my presentation I talked about the group of ports and how they work together and how they needed to work together. It was interesting when we talk about 8 and 10 and 12,000 ton topsides, these big, big topsides that we showed a few pictures of, is a lot of—even if they built at McDermott shore or at Gulf Island's yard or at Dynamics yard. All of the ports, a lot of those facilities, we were in New Iberia, what, a couple of weeks ago, 3 or 4 weeks ago.

A lot of that equipment you saw was going on wells, platforms that were built somewhere else. So a lot of the small pieces, if you when you interview some of the Vermillion port folks, they are subcontractors to the big fabricators. So all of these pieces get put when it looks like it's delivered out of Houma or delivered out of New Iberia when in fact there's a whole number of those smaller ports that need to be connected to those, the infrastructure needs to connect those things, to keep them all. Because when you see a big platform in Houma a lot of those pieces are built in Vermillion and in other areas, in Abbeville and other pieces are built in different places. So it's not just one port.

The CHAIR. Are we building?

Right.

Mr. MALBROUGH. In one little region.

The CHAIR. So it's important.

Also for the redundancy, you know, in the event we get, you know, when you're in a situation like we are in a storm, a frequent storm situation. You literally cannot have all of your rigs in one basket.

Mr. MALBROUGH. Exactly.

The CHAIR. Because you could get into serious trouble if you had all of your rigs or production. So it's important to have that redundancy across the Gulf of Mexico just for that reason and across Louisiana as well.

But do we build? How much of our fabrication is being built here and going overseas? Do we have some of it that's being built here and floated in other parts or is mostly the work that we do here for the Gulf?

I mean, I know most of it is for the Gulf.

Mr. MALBROUGH. Yes.

The CHAIR. But we do some international.

Mr. MALBROUGH. There is in the fabrication side which is generally, the work we do is in channel depth, is centered in and around the fabrication side. There is a lot of equipment and a lot of things that are shipped to the North Sea.

The CHAIR. Yes.

Mr. MALBROUGH. Other areas.

In the Corps of Engineers analysis of the economic boom they used the—a lot of those countries have utilization requirements where the—it looks like it on paper that the equipment is built, has to be built in Nigeria, as an example, in one of these foreign countries.

What happens is you end up having a company there that subs out our local fin. We ship a lot of equipment overseas to those areas that in fact looks like it's done in the Nigeria area, but it's really not. It's on the——

The CHAIR. This is very important testimony to get on the record. I'd like you, Neil, as from representing one of the largest companies in the world to please give us some additional information for that because when we talk about this work being done along the Gulf of Mexico it's not just for the Gulf of Mexico. It's for drilling operations all over the world.

The CHAIR. We know that our technology is used all over the world, clearly, which is a great benefit. But our actual fabrication and equipment that is built here, the steel that comes into our ports is fabricated and used all over the world for drilling. I think sometimes we don't get the credit that we deserve for that because it's not easily dissected in the economic data.

But it's important, again, getting back to what Mr. Leimkuhler said, so we can be more effective advocates for this region. It's not just jobs here. It's jobs all over the United States. It's just not facilities or platforms that we're building and rigs that we're using in the Gulf. This is used all over the world.

So if the world is interested in energy the Federal Government of the United States needs to support the energy coast here in a much more robust way than they are currently doing. That has been my message. We're building a record so that this message can be received and heard in a way that will move a political organization like the Congress to do something about it and not just ignore it and go on with business as usual.

Business as usual is clearly not going to work for the Gulf States. I mean we will not be here if it's business as usual because of the pressures on this coast from a variety of different perspectives. That's not the subject of this hearing, but we all know the coastal challenge to our coastal restoration and marshes that are underway. The challenges to our cities, to Houma, to New Orleans, to Lafayette, to New Iberia, to Delcom, to Lake Charles, to Cameron, Johnson Bayou, etcetera, etcetera, all the way to the tail of Plackman Parish.

Mr. Ramsay, do you have any closing remarks?

Mr. RAMSAY. Yes, with that in mind, you know, this region being so important to energy production here in this country and worldwide, you know, even though this region has a very skilled work force it's an aging one. We're struggling to feed that pipeline. We could use increased funding from the Department of Labor for grants for training, advancement and retention such as, you know, the State incumbent worker program.

You know, these are great jobs. They pay $50, $60, $100,000, you know, in 4 to 5 years for these kids that come straight out of high school. I think, you know, the partnering with the technical and community colleges is important, but we should do more as well.

You know, the STEM is the new education term, science, technology, engineering and math programs, you know, is being touted around by everybody in the country. But those students in our elementary schools and our high schools need to be exposed to this industry. It's a great industry to be involved in. It's a very promising thing.

So any help along those lines will be appreciated.

The CHAIR. Thank you for raising that. The work force issues are just tremendous, the challenges for our area, for the country. We've conducted—I've conducted in a different role as Chair of the Homeland Security Committee and just in an economic development, you know, hat on the challenge for our work force.

Thank you for raising that. It is important.

Mr. Leimkuhler.

Mr. LEIMKUHLER. I guess if I had to close with one closing comment it would be really around the empowerment of the technical staff of the regulators. These are very competent people. But at sometimes when we manage through issues and challenges with them you feel like their hands are tied a little bit.

It's going to be essentially for healthy staff empowered if we were to move to a performance based standard of regulations rather than a prescriptive. You shall do this. You shall do this. You shall do this.

Under a prescriptive regime it doesn't fit every situation. You get into situations where from a risk and a safety standpoint you need a variance. It's difficult sometimes to obtain those because the staff just don't feel as empowered as I think they need to be.

The CHAIR. Excellent.

Mr. Satterlee.

Mr. SATTERLEE. As we move into more frontier areas such as Alaska and the Atlantic and the Eastern Gulf of Mexico it's important to recognize that if we can do it safely then we're confident that changes have been made to prevent another reoccurrence of a blowout, an oil spill. Then we can do it in a way that protects the environment, protects our personnel.

Second, from an economic standpoint Shell has spent over $5 billion in Alaska so far. We still don't have our permits. If all the building blocks are put in place and we're able to get our permits and we have a discovery that's only going to be a sliver of what our company and other companies will spend in the development of the Arctic.

The same holds true in other frontier areas.

In Alaska what we found was a very large amount of what we spent came from Louisiana. We built 2, at least 2, OSVs right here in Louisiana. Much of our man power came from Louisiana, a lot of the equipment.

We'll see the same thing in the Atlantic. They just don't have those kind of capabilities on the Atlantic Coast. So much of that will have to come from the Gulf Coast.

The CHAIR. So the opportunity for opening Alaska, opening the Atlantic Coast, the opening of Mexico, is going to position Louisiana to be an extraordinary provider.

Mr. SATTERLEE. Right.

The CHAIR. Of technology, equipment, personnel. But the challenges, work force, infrastructure, regulatory regime, and just basic investments. So they are great opportunities, but they are great challenges. Thank you all very much for contributing to this record.

The field hearing is adjourned.

[Whereupon, at 3:40 p.m. the hearing was adjourned.]

○